ISRAEL *and* TOMORROW'S TEMPLE

ISRAEL *and* TOMORROW'S TEMPLE

By
THOMAS S. McCALL
and
ZOLA LEVITT

MOODY PRESS
CHICAGO

Original title: *Satan in the Sanctuary*

© 1973, 1977, by
THE MOODY BIBLE INSTITUTE
OF CHICAGO

All rights reserved

Printed in the United States of America

Contents

CHAPTER		PAGE
	Foreword	7
	Preface	9
	Introduction to the Revised Edition	13
1.	Another Temple—So What?	19
2.	The Stage Is Set	22
3.	Opening Pandora's Box—Prayer on the Mount	39
4.	The Jerusalem Great Synagogue—A Halfway House?	56
5.	Step by Step—A Plan of Action	66
6.	The Bible Tells Me So	77
7.	Moses to Moshe—A Bloody Site	90
8.	I Will Fill This House with Glory	107
9.	The Antichrist—"War I Give unto You"	130
10.	The End Times—A Timetable	139
11.	The Truth Will Set You Free	153
	Notes	158

Taken during the recent filming on location in Jerusalem of "The Temple," a major new film based on this book, this picture shows the authors Zola Levitt (right) and Dr. Thomas McCall (left) on a balcony overlooking the famed temple site. The Wailing Wall, one of the few visible remains of the ancient temple, where devout Jews come can be seen in the background. The Dome of the Rock, a Moslem mosque which now occupies much of the temple site, is located just behind the Wailing Wall.

"The Temple," produced by Mal Couch and the Evangelical Communications Research Foundation, is available at your nearest Christian film distributor. Don't miss this powerful film!

Foreword

FROM THE DIVINE VIEWPOINT, Jerusalem has always been the center of the stage of world history. In all probability, Melchisedec, to whom Abraham paid tithes, was king there. According to the Tell el Amarna tablets discovered in Egypt, Jerusalem was in existence at least in the fifteenth century B.C. Abraham was instructed to offer Isaac on Mount Moriah, near where the Temple of Solomon was to be built a thousand years later (2 Ch 3:1). Jerusalem was made the capital of the kingdom of Israel by David and Solomon, and there the tabernacle was given a permanent home. Acting on instructions from God, Solomon built the magnificent Temple that stood for centuries until destroyed by the Babylonians in 586 B.C. The Temple was rebuilt in Jerusalem by the returning captives from Babylon seventy years after Solomon's Temple was destroyed. Finally, Herod constructed a magnificent new Temple in Jerusalem, begun about 20 B.C. and completed in A.D. 64.

After the destruction of Jerusalem and Herod's Temple in A.D. 70, Jerusalem ceased to be the center of Israel's national life until our generation. The return of Israel as a nation—symbolized by their organization as a political state in May 1948—and the dramatic repossession of the city in 1967 are tremendously significant events. They have made Jerusalem once again the capital of Israel and have set the stage for the erection of the next Temple to be built in Israel before the coming of Christ to establish His kingdom on earth.

This volume effectively presents the prophetic Scriptures yet to be fulfilled, including those concerning the magnificent Temple in the millennial kingdom, when Jerusalem will be the capital of the world and Christ will reign over every nation.

Contemporary events point to the conclusion that we are moving rapidly to this end-time situation. This book dramatically captures history and prophecy as they relate to Jerusalem and the Temple. It should fascinate every reader and constitute a pointed reminder that the coming of Christ for His church is imminent.

JOHN F. WALVOORD

Preface

PEOPLE HAVE ALWAYS WONDERED about the future, but nowadays that natural wonder is turning into concern. Where are we going? What lies ahead? What is the world coming to?

There has been a heightened interest in present-day prophets who claim to foresee important events in the future of politics or war, and in astrologers who seem to specialize in our emotional futures. But whatever the particular medium, the concern is real.

There has also been an enormous surge of interest in biblical prophecy as a means of seeing the future. Today it's not just the isolated Bible scholar or seminary student who is knowledgeable in the visions of Daniel and the Revelation; the man on the street is becoming informed.

A number of important books have been produced which explain the general conclusions of biblical prophecy, including Hal Lindsey's *The Late, Great Planet Earth,* and they have promoted a justifiable attention to the Bible as a tool of understanding world events and their direction.

The Bible has been around for a long time and has always been appreciated at least for its literature, if not its message. But lately, there's a new appreciation. As world conditions progress, people have begun to notice that the Bible has something to say about them.

One is reminded of Mark Twain's humorous comment about his father. "When I was fourteen," he reminisced, "I discovered that my father was so dumb it was embarrassing to have him around. When I was twenty-one, I was amazed at what he'd learned in seven years."

The Bible has seemed to learn a great deal lately. The restoration of Israel, the creation of the Common Market, the Six-Day War, the alignment of Russia against Israel, the ecumenical church movement, the prevalence of earthquakes, and many other major developments on the world scene are all prophesied in the Bible. What's more, all of these are given as signs of the end times. It is as though the stage is being set for the final outworkings of God's plan for mankind. World events are falling into place like the pieces of a gigantic puzzle.

This book confines itself to the possibilities of the rebuilding of the Jerusalem Temple, a prophecy which has come into sharp focus since the Six-Day War, in which Israel recovered the ancient Temple site in the Old City of Jerusalem. The prophecies concerning this event are examined in detail and compared with the current scene in the Holy Land. The world-shaking importance of this piece of that gigantic puzzle is emphasized.

The authors have brought together theological and journalistic experience to present in clear form the appearance of one of those signs of the end times. Dr. McCall originally gave the ideas included here in an article published in *Bibliotheca Sacra*, "How Soon the Tribulation Temple?" (Fall, 1971; Spring, 1972).

It is the hope of the authors to reach all readers, believers in Christ and unbelievers alike, with the message that God's Word goes on, oblivious to doubt, and that we alive today are in a position to see it fulfilled.

Preface

May the readers of this book be drawn to faith in the God who controls all history and makes all prophecy come to pass, and in His Son, the Lord Jesus Christ.

Introduction
to the Revised Edition

IT IS OVERWHELMINGLY EXCITING to see that a book on Bible prophecy released in the latter part of 1973 already needs a revised edition!

The revisions contained in this volume do not have to do with corrections of fact or more depth of research. This book is devoted to real progress toward the fulfillment of prophecy. God has perceptively moved since 1973 to bring ever closer the reality of the Tribulation Temple.

Those privileged to watch prophecy fulfilled throughout history lived in most exciting times. Imagine the drama in Babylon when the prophet Daniel was able to announce the end of the captivity of Israel in the sixth century before Christ. He had seen the prophecy (Jer 29:10), and then the people were to see the promised freedom actually worked out by God. Imagine the astonishment of those knowledgeable in prophecy about the Messiah observing the carpenter of Galilee fulfilling it all as He traveled in their land.

In our own times, the recovery of Israel by the chosen people has privileged us to stand in the wings as the stage is set for God's grand finale, the return of Christ to the earth, and the establishment of the Kingdom of God. The 1967 Six-Day War returned the site of the ancient Temples of God to the Jews, and this return paved the way for the consideration of a new Temple for the coming tribulation period.

It appears that we are nearing the "end times" of Bible

prophecy as we watch enormous upheavals of a religious and political nature throughout the world. The coming rapture of the Church needs no signs to precede it, according to prophecy, but we are seeing the preparation of the tribulation which is to immediately follow the rapture. We indeed are privileged.

It should be realized that we could have lived at any time through the past nineteen centuries and not seen the slightest hint of progress toward the rebuilding of the Temple of God in Jerusalem. In all of that time the Jewish people were in dispersion, away from the promised land. But now, in God's providence, they are home again, and, we can see they are getting ready to rebuild the Temple.

The ongoing drama of the Temple Mount in Jerusalem certainly bears close scrutiny for those who believe the precise declarations of the Bible. It is there that most of the prophecy of our times and the end times will unfold. The Temple must be rebuilt at some point prior to the middle of the seven-year period of tribulation. It must be rebuilt on its appointed site, the site of its forerunners, the Temples of Solomon and Herod. We must watch, but very carefully; distinguishing between fact and rumor and between wishful thinking and accurate observation. We must not misread events, either through insensitivity to prophecy or over-anticipation of its fulfillment.

After the Six-Day War the chosen people began to conduct archaeological research around the Temple Mount, and this slow-going but dramatic work has begun to uncover the secrets of the Temple worship of the past. When the new Temple is built, the Jews will be ready to use it. We were able to report in the original edition, *Satan in the Sanctuary*, that much of the underground geography of the former Temples had been uncovered and many valuable artifacts found.

Introduction to the Revised Edition 15

The archaeology goes on, but we can now add to it many other startling developments leading toward the fulfillment of the prophecy of end times in obvious ways.

First and foremost, there have been the political developments which have virtually changed the world in a few short years. The 1973 War, the Yom Kippur War, with its accompanying Arab oil embargo, has made Israel a focal point of tension among the global powers. The increasing unrest in the Middle East leads directly toward the most foreboding consequences of the coming tribulation.

Second, the archaeology has progressed now to the point where the Israelis are working on an "archaeological park" at the Temple site, open to the peoples of the world who visit Israel. The ancient Temple settings have been uncovered to a great degree, and artifacts have been found from vastly differing periods. Roman coins and relics from the period following the destruction of the second Temple lie open to inspection now, and far below them relics have been uncovered from the period of the Israeli kings during the first Temple times. An Egyptian idol has been found dating to the period of the paganized King Ahaz. With the relics, of course, comes much information that the scholars are able to use in planning for the accurate placement and construction of the third Temple, the coming Tribulation Temple.

Next in the line of developments since our original publication must come the renewed interest of the true church in this prophecy. *Satan in the Sanctuary* had an unpredictably large and lengthy distribution through its various editions by Moody Press, Bantam Books, and German and Finnish translations—over two hundred thousand copies. What was once a rather obscure issue of prophecy has now come to light, so that Christians everywhere are deeply knowledgeable about the coming Temple in Jerusalem. This, in turn, has had an effect on tourism to Israel to see the Temple site, much teaching in the churches, and new books on the Temple issue.

The film, *The Temple,* produced by Evangelical Communications Research Foundation, with the authors serving as technical consultant and writer-actor respectively, has also had a very wide distribution, being shown in thousands of churches and before Christian groups throughout the world. It pinpoints the prophecies concerning the Temple, and it shows the actual locations in Israel where the prophecy is expected to see its ultimate fulfillment.

The past few years have also seen legal and religious struggles over the presence of evangelical Christianity in the Jewish homeland. But there have, too, issued forth the beginnings of meaningful communication between the true Church in Europe and the United States and the citizenry of Israel. There are now strong ties between the leadership of the Church and that of the promised land.

We have also seen a development hard to anticipate in view of the tense political situation between the Jews and the Moslems. We have seen in the past three years the approach of prayerful Jews to the Temple Mount itself. Of course, the Dome of the Rock and the El Aksa Mosque, important Muslim shrines, now stand on the mount, and the Jews normally worship at the Western Wall below. But small groups of Jewish worshipers have actually gone up to the surface, in the face of the strongest Moslem objections, and held organized Jewish prayer—the first on the surface of the mount since A.D. 70!

We have also seen the undertaking of the construction of the Jerusalem Great Synagogue, a magnificent central shrine of world Jewry, to be set in the New City of Jerusalem near the Temple mount. The Great Synagogue has been compared

Introduction to the Revised Edition 17

and contrasted to the coming Temple by many prophecy analysts.

Finally, we have also seen, since the publication of our original book, the published intentions of a minority of Jewish people to rebuild the Temple now, despite any obstacles, even the formidable pressures of Arab objection and global unease about provocations in the Middle East.

The last three of the above developments are taken up in detail in this new edition. They truly update the progress of a prophecy fulfillment, we feel, and they contain vital new issues which strongly suggest biblical overtones. They truly move toward the finale of God's plan for men.

As we go on in our fortunate situation of being able to observe God's Word in action, we cannot help but dedicate ourselves and our work to the even more vital issues of the Bible. The Tribulation Temple, in all its glory, is but a Temple for a season. This book explains that it will be swept away when the Lord returns. Believers will see yet a fourth Temple on the holy site, the Millennial Temple, the central house of Jesus Christ on the earth.

Our continuing prayer is that this book will share in the drawing of men and women around the world to the Lord Jesus Christ, the true Object of all prophecy, and will alert Christians to the strategic nature of the times in which we live.

As the return of the Lord draws near, the importance of displaying every detail of God's Word to a lost world becomes ever more vital. May this book, in its way, contribute to that greatest of all causes.

1

Another Temple—So What?

June, 1967.

An Israeli paratrooper, machine gun in hand, leaps through narrow passageways, sobbing with emotion. He hurls himself against a wall—the Wailing Wall, remnant of Herod's great Jerusalem Temple. Within these walls had stood the ancient priests of biblical Judaism. And here, too, once stood Jesus Christ, preaching the Word of God.

The soldier was running in footprints going back through millennia. Egyptian troops, Assyrians, Babylonians, Romans, Arabians, crusading Europeans, Turks, the British, and modern Arabs, had all contested this battle-scarred, thirty-four-acre property. For 3,000 years wars have raged in dispute over the Temple site.

What for?

Previous conquerors wanted control of the crossroads of the Middle East, but the most significant answer is what will happen in the future on this real estate. True enough, the site has always had great significance. God wanted His great first Temple built exactly on this spot. On this spot he tested His faithful follower Abraham with the hardest of all tests—the sacrifice of his only son. Then He passed the test Himself—sending His only Son, the Christ, into that same Temple mount to be ridiculed and sentenced to crucifixion.

With forewarnings from His great Hebrew prophets, God had the holy Temple built and destroyed twice over, on this same piece of ground.

The Moslems had almost as much regard for that singular site as the Jews before them. They constructed their mighty Dome of the Rock, a strikingly beautiful place of worship, and have maintained it there for thirteen centuries. It stands squarely on the Temple site today. They too had war—with the Crusaders of Europe who were determined to rescue God's hallowed ground from desecration. In the twelfth century the Christians from Europe used the Dome as a church, relinquishing it finally to hordes of Moslems in a ferocious holy war.

But all of that is just a series of mild disagreements compared to what is coming. The Temple site is about to play its greatest role. It will host the most bestial monster the world has ever known. And then it will be a major issue of Armageddon.

The final chapters of the earth's political, military, and religious history will revolve around the site of the ancient Temples. A splendid new Temple, the equal of those past illustrious houses of God, will rise on the site. A powerful and engaging world leader will pose a peace formula for Israel and will eventually turn himself into a terrible dictator. His fanaticism will exceed Hitler's. He will proclaim himself God in the Temple, and he will demand the worship of all humanity. He will embroil the entire world in war such as never has been imagined. All past and present wars together would not be the equal of this coming holocaust.

The Jerusalem Temple will be stage-center as usual.

Another Temple—So What?

But this great war will signal the second coming of our Lord Jesus Christ. "Unless those days are shortened [by My return] all mankind will perish," He observed sadly in Matthew 24:22 (*Living Bible*). Christ will sweep away this new Temple—the Tribulation Temple—and replace it with His own house on the earth.

We will show in this book how the stage has been set; how the great biblical prophets, whose accuracy has already been demonstrated, have foreseen all of these developments; how the end of the world will be.

It is vital—now that Temple reconstruction plans may well be underway—for every living person to understand this culmination of world history. It is vital for all of us to face up to the Word of God and realize that it has been, and will be, fulfilled. It is vital that we all know the most important truth of our times—that God's plan will prevail.

By a complete understanding of this truth, men can yet see the tragedies to come, and God's provision for escape.

"And ye shall know the truth, and the truth shall make you free" (Jn 8:32).

Another Temple—so what? So everything.

Read on.

2

The Stage Is Set

ONLY JESUS COULD intentionally fulfill prophecy. On several occasions in His ministry He specified that an action was to fulfill prophecy. We cannot cause prophecy to be fulfilled, but we are certainly able to look into the Word and draw conclusions about how it is being fulfilled around us.

June 7, 1967—the day the lethally competent Israeli army overran the ancient Temple site—may have been one of those days which fulfills the prophetic Word. The "times of the Gentiles" (Lk 21:24) may have started to come to an end on that day when the Jews truly "came home" after nearly two thousand years.

What an electric scene that recapture must have been! The last Jewish troops to defend the Temple, in A.D. 70, fought with swords and spears. Now their brethren came with grenades and automatic rifles to reclaim God's chosen site.

Some troops didn't know exactly where to look for the Western Wall as the enemy fled. Many Jews had not been allowed in the area for twenty years. The famous Israeli tourist guides were pressed into service to lead the exhausted soldiers to the hallowed place.

The Stage Is Set

Soon the government leaders were there, and the rabbis. The news spread fast throughout Israel. God had brought His chosen people back to the wall.

And now, perhaps, the new Temple—the third Jerusalem Temple—the Tribulation Temple—could reasonably be spoken of as a possibility.

"As long as the Old City [Jerusalem area containing the Temple site] was in Jordanian hands, the ancient dream of a rebuilt Temple could conveniently be left in the category of dreams," pointed out a recent editorial in *Christianity Today* magazine. "But with the union of all Jerusalem under Jewish control, the dream assumed realistic outlines, and the challenge to rebuild the Temple, with its host of difficult political and religious questions, loomed large."[1]

We must realize the profound difference between the present times and the passage of the centuries since A.D. 70, the destruction of the second Temple. For nearly nineteen centuries there had been no reasonable hint of the Tribulation Temple prophecies being fulfilled. The Jews had been scattered like grains of sand in a hurricane. The world was filled with the Jews, in the respect that they resided everywhere from Siberia to Kansas in those nineteen centuries. They could hardly look objectively to reconstructing their Temple. They pled with God four times a week to "renew our days as they once were." Their patience and faith is only equalled by that of the Christians awaiting the return of the Lord.

But now, since 1948, there has been a dramatic turn of events. The Jews now have their promised land, and with it all the possibilities of things becoming "as they once were."

And since 1967, they hold the actual site of their ancient Temple.

24   *Israel and Tomorrow's Temple*

One is reminded of the succinct prophecy of our Lord in Luke 21:24 which reviews this situation: "And they shall fall by the edge of the sword, and shall be led away captive into all nations: and Jerusalem shall be trodden down of the Gentiles, until the times of the Gentiles be fulfilled."

The scope of our Lord's foreknowledge is breathtaking. The prophecy has clearly been justified. The Jews hold the Temple site, and in the words of their brilliant military commander Moshe Dayan, "No power on earth will remove us from this spot again."

And rebuilding the Temple at this time has not escaped the Jews as a real possibility. Rabbi Sinai Halberstam, writing in *The Jewish Press,* August 2, 1968, noted, "When Jerusalem was in foreign hands the question always arose, 'When can we rebuild our beloved Temple?' Even more so does this question arise today when, with the blessing of the Almighty, Jerusalem has been returned to the caretaking of Jewish hands. The Temple grounds are again under the control of the descendants of those who stood upon Mount Sinai. When will the Temple be rebuilt?"[2]

Time magazine, ordinarily no valuable source of biblical commentary, speculated on the possibilities only one month after the Six-Day War, and published an article entitled "Should the Temple be Rebuilt?" On June 30, 1967, that potent secular periodical asked, "Assuming that Israel keeps the Western Wall, which is one of the few remaining ruins of Judaism's Second Temple, has the time now come for the erection of the Third Temple?"[3]

An Israeli guide reports that he attended the recent rededication of the restored main Jewish Synagogue in the Jewish quarter in Old Jerusalem, with hundreds of Israelis present. The officiating rabbi stirred the crowd by predicting, "As the city has been reunited in our lifetime, so

The Stage Is Set 25

will the rebuilding of the Temple be accomplished in our lifetime!"

The *Time* article goes on to review the nineteen centuries of hope that have passed among the scattered Jews, and says, "Although Zionism was largely a secular movement, one of its sources was the prayers of Jews for a return to Palestine so that they could rebuild a new Temple."[4]

Looking at the 1967 situation, *Time* went on to say,

> Such is Israel's euphoria today that some Jews see plausible theological grounds for discussing reconstruction. They base their argument on the contention that Israel has already entered its "Messianic Era" (the time of the coming of the Jewish Messiah, as expected in Jewish theology.) In 1948, they note, Israel's chief rabbis ruled that with the establishment of the Jewish state and the ingathering of the exiles, the age of redemption had begun.
>
> Today many of Israel's religious leaders are convinced that the Jews' victory over the Arabs has taken Judaism well beyond that point. Says historian Israel Eldad: "We are at the stage where David was when he liberated Jerusalem. From that time until the construction of the Temple by Solomon, only one generation passes. So will it be with us." And what about that Moslem shrine? [standing directly on the Temple site?] Answers Eldad: "It is of course an open question. Who knows? Perhaps there will be an earthquake."[5]

Fascinating. Our time is compared to that of David and Solomon, when all Israel focused on the construction of the splendid first Temple. And perhaps God will act to clear the site. This has been the generation of liberation comparable to the coming of David's armies. The next generation, as the Jewish scholar sees it, will be like that of Solomon—the actual building.

Concerning the current scene in Israel, there are many indications that reconstruction of the Temple is a very real possibility. The authors were able to interview two eyewitnesses of the diggings at the Temple Mount, who noted peculiar happenings as the work progresses.

Dr. Roy Blizzard, a professional archaeologist on the faculty at the University of Texas, has participated in the archaeological work at the site since its inception in 1968. Blizzard has worked with Dr. Benjamin Mazar of the Hebrew University at Jerusalem, who heads the project.

Dr. Blizzard said,

> Dr. Mazar told me this past summer (1972) that there would be another five years' work in the Temple site before they would even think of quitting the excavations. The archaeological crews have been working steadily on a year-round basis throughout the four years, and they have uncovered much evidence of the history of the Western and Southern Walls of the Temple area going back to the days of Herod's and even Solomon's Temple.
>
> There have been articles in archaeological journals about the work, but there seems to be a reluctance on the part of the excavators to discuss the Temple area because of the political pressures which can be generated by the rabbinate. This is in contrast with the general openness about other Israeli excavations.
>
> The public can see the excavations from a distance, but only the archaeological workers, VIP's, and people with special authorizations can walk through the site. Some of the tunnels underneath the Temple mount have been excavated to a certain point, and then blockaded with wooden barriers. The tunnels have been closed because of political overtones, and the sacredness of the Temple area.

The Stage Is Set

Why such controversy about archaeological findings?

Universally, archeologists are eager to demonstrate what they have found, and to publish their discoveries. This has been true at other diggings in Israel.

But, we suggest, the Temple site has a character of importance about it not wholly attributable to its sacredness. We suggest that the idea of reconstruction underlies the controversy noted by Blizzard.

The authors also talked with an Israeli guide who has also been down in the diggings. The guide accompanied Mazar, and also Rabbi Dov Perla, director of the Israeli Government Department of Sacred Sites and Antiquities of the Ministry of Religion, in the latter's excavations of the northerly section of the Western Wall. He gives an account of the findings in the diggings which may serve to give an appreciation of the past Temples:

> Digging through portions of the Western and Southern walls the excavators found an intriguing network of tunnels underground. I have examined them. One of them appears to be a passageway for the ancient high priest to pass from his living quarters to the Court of the Priests. This tunnel was of particular importance on the day of atonement when the high priest could not defile himself by contact with other people. In his task of atoning for all of the Jews he had to be completely pure and undefiled on that day. But other tunnels were not for human passage, but for water drainage. This was extremely sophisticated. Solomon's and Herod's Temples contained intricate systems for storing water and carrying it away from the Temple site to the adjacent Kidron Valley. The ancient "Laver" or "Sea", the great bronze bowl standing before the Temple, had to be drained and replenished regularly with vast quantities of water. Also, the altar of

sacrifice, which collected the blood of sacrificed animals and the burned remains, had to be washed down and flushed clean by the priests every night. These facilities required quite a drainage system for their times. I was in the water drainage tunnels, and I was able to stand upright. They are more than six feet in height. It has been estimated that the total water that was stored in cisterns and reservoirs within the Temple mount amounted to 10 million gallons.

Also discovered in the diggings have been clues to information about weights and measures lost for millennia. The law of Moses requires a strict system of these weights and measures as regards Temple worship. Grain and other offerings must be reckoned very exactly, and the precise value of many of the recorded weights and measures had been buried for 1900 years. Many people wondered how these important provisions of the law could be observed even if the Temple were rebuilt at once. But the excavations uncovered coins and stone weights with Hebrew inscriptions on them. Some of these go back to prehistoric times. The exact weight of a "sheckel" is now known, as well as other important weights and measures. And of course the excavations have only begun.

Also uncovered now are the steps to the Huldah Gate through the south wall. These were undoubtedly the steps used by Jesus and the apostles when they ascended to the Temple. The Huldah Gate was used by the common people coming to worship, as opposed to the gates on the Western Wall, which were used by priests and royalty.

The guide notes another phenomenon in Israel concerning the Temple site work:

> A great and cohesive body of knowledge is being collected about the past Temples, and new discoveries are

being added to it regularly. In the Yeshivas and the halls of Jewish learning, Temple knowledge is being emphasized, with a view to educating the people in proper Temple worship. There is a real excitement apparent.

While this interest is very natural in the light of the new discoveries, it is not limited to mere pride of heritage. Supposing for a moment that a new Temple were actually to be constructed soon, would the Israeli people, who have not participated in authentic Temple worship, have a proper knowledge and appreciation for it?

We suggest that some of this heightened interest and scholarship has a very practical basis. Temple worship is exacting and detailed. We suggest that the people are being educated to understand it properly when the third Jerusalem Temple is ready.

Illustrating more directly the controversy surrounding this issue is the July, 1972 issue of the "Yanetz" Prayer Letter. This newsletter, published in Jerusalem by Christians, quotes in turn the March 21, 1972, issue of the MaAriv newspaper, which gives an account of a real reconstruction attempt:

> Since the 6 Day War we have heard many rumors and false reports regarding the rebuilding of the Temple in Jerusalem, that even stones were being cut in America, all of which is completely untrue. But we now have just seen the first signs or glimmer of tangible interest by a group of Israeli Jews who seriously want to have the Temple rebuilt. We indicate excerpts from the 21 March 72 issue of MaAriv newspaper which we believe is important in light of our current world situation: "An Othomanical Association for the Rebuilding of the Temple Receives No Permit from the Ministry of the Internal Affairs."

"Five young Jewish Israelis from different backgrounds, vocations and parts of Israel sat conversing passionately last summer and were united with one common and strong desire, expressed by the words of the prayer, 'Let the Temple be rebuilt, soon in our lifetime.' For these five men, the words of this prayer are more than just mere wishful thinking. They want to turn that hidden longing into reality as they said, 'Let us help in rebuilding the Temple.'

"These five initiators understand that they cannot do all the work alone, neither physically nor financially, since they have families and must continue in their jobs. But led by Rabbi Tarfon's saying (*Pirke Abot*), 'You don't have to finish the whole work, but you are not excused from doing it.' So these five thought it will be enough if they can hold up the banner for others to follow.

"Five members formed an Association with program and goals clearly stated: To be in Jerusalem, to organize the leaders of Judiasm and rabbis to study the laws and commandments concerning the rebuilding of the Temple and help to fund the project for donations raised for the rebuilding of the Temple.

"Also, to help in the work of planning and rebuilding and to see that this work is delivered into the hands of architects, engineers, artists, fine craftsmen, masons, smiths and carpenters. All these specialists are to be organized by the Association. It was noted that much money will be required for the above purpose and so it was established that the Association would have the right to purchase and erect branches all over the country and world to collect funds to further their goals.

"The first application for official registry was refused by the Ministry of Interior but the five initiators are appealing to the Supreme Court emphasizing, 'The purposes

The Stage Is Set

of the Association are legitimate.' But the refusal of the man in charge to register the Association contradicts the longing of those who pray, 'And may our eyes behold the return to Zion in mercy.' It is also an active commandment to build the Temple in Jerusalem and everyone is obliged to help build it whether physically or financially. Now since the Temple area is in Jewish sovereign control, no further delay should be tolerated, but all must act towards this building of the Temple. The founders say that there are all the ancient classes of Israel among our number: Priests, Levites and Israelites. They long to behold the Holy Temple gloriously erected on its ancient site. All must be done to allow it according to the Law of Israel. They also believe that the Association's work will create a wide echo.

"This application was registered with the Supreme Court of Justice a few days before Passover Eve and the man in charge of the Jerusalem district was asked to explain why he should not retract this rejection to the registration of the Association for the rebuilding of the Temple in Jerusalem."

We hope that the information in the above article will better enable you to pray for our Lord's work in our land of Israel. It is becoming more and more evident that the hour is growing late! Please pray for us in this hour![6]

The hour surely appears to be growing late. Will an application for official registry be approved soon?

Well, it's not as easy as all that. There is a four-sided controversy going on over the Temple possibilities at present—with the Moslems, the Christians, the Jews, and God all having something to say. Here, in brief, are the various positions.

WHAT THE MOSLEMS SAY

The Moslem shrine, the Dome of the Rock, is no small matter to the Moslems. The Arabs will certainly not stand by while their shrine is removed. And the Jews will not disturb it on principle; it is an Israeli law not to disturb any site sacred to any religion.

The Jews know best of any people how tragic it is to have the symbols of faith desecrated.

The Dome of the Rock, as the shrine is called, and the nearby El Aksa Mosque, stand squarely on the site. The Dome is no late-comer among religious shrines, having been completed by the Mohammedans in A.D. 691. They cared for it respectfully, doing extensive repairs and restorations over the centuries. During the Crusades they met the hordes of Europe in horribly bloody battles over the site, losing their shrine for a century on one occasion. The Christian invaders used the Dome of the Rock as a Christian church for this time, but the Mohammedans retook it and have maintained it ever since.

It is fair to say that in struggle and longevity, the Dome of the Rock compares favorably with the two Jewish Temples. And the Arabs have at least as much determination as the Jews to hold onto the same piece of ground.

The Arab world went into a frenzy in 1969 when an Australian Christian set fire to the El Aksa Mosque in an attempt to help God fulfill His prophecies. Things would be quite a bit smoother if the Jews built their new Temple across town, but unfortunately the law is very clear. Deuteronomy 12:10-14 and 2 Samuel 24:16-19 ("a place which the LORD your God shall choose") leave no doubt that God is sensitive to the exact location of the Temple and will have it where it stood before.

What the Christians Say

Another obstacle to the rebuilding comes from Christian sources. Some Christians object to the idea of a new Temple on the grounds that the death of Christ was sufficient atonement, and the Levitical system of offering sacrifices to God has no further use. They would have difficulty accepting the idea of a revived Temple complete with sacrifices.

However, as the next chapter explains in detail, the Bible teaches that there will be two future Temples—the Tribulation Temple, and then Christ's Millennial Temple. And Temples mean sacrifices (2 Ch 7:12). In the Tribulation Temple, sacrifices will be offered by unbelieving Israel, and God will apparently allow the worship in His permissive will.[7] In the Millennial Temple, established by the Lord Himself, the sacrifices will likely be of a memorial nature, commemorating His atoning work on the cross.[8]

WHAT THE JEWS SAY

But there are Jewish objections. Only the Messiah can rebuild the Temple, say some Jewish theologians. And He hasn't come yet, according to their view.

This argument centers around whether the Messiah must personally gather the Jews and rebuild the Temple and its worship systems, or whether the idea of this being the Messianic Age is sufficient grounds to go ahead.

Official rabbinical law presently forbids the Jews to touch the site. When the Israeli troops overran the site during the Six-Day War, the chief rabbi of Jerusalem immediately put up a sign admonishing the Jews to stay out of the Temple area proper, lest they desecrate the most holy place.

By this thinking, no Orthodox Jewish bricklayer or carpenter will go beyond the Western Wall, even if the site were prepared—with the Dome out of the way. There is some Talmudic support for the Messiah having to do the job in person, but the matter is not completely clear. In any case, serious objections among the theological powers that be in Jerusalem constitute a major obstacle to the rebuilding.

Standing in the way of immediate reconstruction also is the lack of a proper priesthood to staff the place. The Old Testament priesthood is extinct, or at least dormant.

Not just anybody can officiate in the Jewish Temple. An unimpeachable pedigree and strict regulations bore upon the Temple priests of the past in order that they be fit for their ministries. The spirit was continued in the New Testament, where Christians are admonished to be "holy vessels" for their Lord.

But in a certain sense the Jewish priesthood has survived the ages. The Jewish Encyclopedia says that there are Jews named Cohen in plentiful numbers today, who claim to be descendants of Aaron, the first high priest (*Cohen* means "priests" in Hebrew.) In Jewish life, the Cohens, as well as the Levites (names *Levy, Levine,* etc.) enjoy certain privileges. They are chosen as the first to read the Scriptures in the synagogues, and they officiate at Jewish functions, as is traditional. They also have certain ritual responsibilities.[9]

Conceivably then, the priestly robes might be handed down, and the present-day Cohens and Levites might serve in the roles of their honored ancestors in the third Temple.

Still another Jewish objection to the rebuilding has to do with the reestablishment of the old Temple practices. Sacrifice, in the form of killing animals in the Temple, is abhorrent to much modern Jewish thought. The Temple might well be built, but most Jews, especially Reform Jews, will not entertain the thought of what they call "slaughter house religion" or "primitive ritual," and this would certainly affect the fulfillment of the prophecies about the Tribulation Temple.

For the building simply to be constructed and used for nonsacrificial worship would not completely identify with the Scriptures about the third Temple. The Antichrist must abolish the sacrifices and oblations. If they are not there, we would have just another modern Jewish synagogue, albeit standing at the right place.

What God Says

So there are Moslem, Christian, and Jewish objections to the immediate construction of the Tribulation Temple. And on the other side is the Word of God. A great deal must be overcome on earth for God's Word to be fulfilled, but that has been the case in many instances before. Chapter 3 reviews in detail what God has indicated in His Word concerning the future of the Temple site. God's Word has the last word.

The Earthly Incentives

We might look a moment at the brighter side of this picture. There are many earthly incentives for the Temple to be built soon.

Among Bible-believing Christians, of course, is the idea of fulfilling prophecy. The great prophecies of Daniel, the Lord, the apostle Paul, and John will be largely fulfilled by the reconstruction itself. It would serve as a faith-building confirmation that the Word of God is still being worked out, and that the scene is being set, as the New Testament promises, for the return of Jesus Christ.

The second benefit to the Christians would be in the matter of witnessing for Christ to the Jews. This is certainly a vital part of the Lord's Great Commission, and one that is very difficult in today's world.

The Jew today is different from his first-century ancestor in that he knows little of the basic biblical issues of sacrifice, the priesthood, and, of course, the fulfillment of these types in Christ, the Jewish Messiah. It is difficult now to refer to the epistle to the Hebrews, designed for the biblically knowledgeable Jews of that time. Today's Jew is simply without the background to appreciate the apostle's point of view. Rabbinic teachings have supplanted these basic issues until they have been all but forgotten.

But if there were an authentic Temple in Jerusalem the Jew could more easily understand what is meant by sacrifice and by priesthood. He could then also be expected to understand atonement and redemption through Christ more readily.

Peter and Paul witnessed to Jews who had the vivid types of Christ inherent in Temple practices right before their eyes. What a harvest there might be if once again these long-suffering servants of God could see objectively the grand traditions of their Temple and their ultimate fulfillment in Christ!

Then there are incentives to the Jews themselves, just as they are, to rebuild their sacred Temple. The first of these is the wonderful answer to nineteen hundred years of prayer. After these millennia of persecution and agony, what a blessing it would be for the Jew to have his house of worship as in the time of Solomon. "Next year in Jerusalem," the great Passover prayer, would be a reality every year!

Second, it would readily bring the Jews to Israel, as well as a lot of Christians. Tourism is a modern concept, but it is one of the important bases of the Israeli economy, and

The Stage Is Set

thus has a great influence on this small nation's place in the world. A central Temple could attract many Jews of the world to make at least one pilgrimage to their ancient holy land. Jews obedient to the laws of Moses would want to go three times a year for the grand feasts—Passover, Pentecost, and Tabernacles. Immigration also would doubtless increase. At present there are 3 million Jews in Israel and 3 million Jews in New York City. The other 7 million are still dispersed throughout the world. Israel needs more of its own.

Third, there would be a political factor—stabilization of the state—inherent in the rebuilding of the Temple. Looking back at the ancient days of the first Temple, we find Jeroboam breaking away and creating the Northern Kingdom, and stopping pilgrimages to the Jerusalem Temple. In 1 Kings 12:27-30 Jeroboam demanded his people in the north to worship in his substitute temples in Beth-el and Dan, and to forget about the Jerusalem Temple. What a dividing and weakening influence this had on the Jewish nation!

Today's divisions and weaknesses are still more obvious. The Jews are indomitable and unrelenting; they have remained Jews in name and practice through some of the most heartless and continuous persecution in the history of man. But they have been divided and on the run for millennia. How much better it would be for them to meet at their Jerusalem Temple once again. How much more significance Israel would have among the nations of the world, if Jews everywhere were united in their common Temple worship.

What Will Happen?

So there are good incentives, as well as formidable obstacles to the construction of the Tribulation Temple. God has laid out quite a puzzle indeed. His chosen people need their Temple and want it. They have historical and biblical precedent to build their Temple now, besides a host of modern practical reasons. But some of them await their Messiah to lead the project and do not favor going ahead.

Then there's the Lord's flock, the Christians, promised the kingdom of heaven. Some of them also want this Temple to be rebuilt, though others demur and say it is contrary to Christ's fulfillment of the sacrifices.

And then we have the Moslems whose mighty shrine has dominated the site chosen by God for thirteen hundred years. They will not allow their Dome of the Rock to be moved. They will doubtless take up arms if there is the slightest threat to it.

And finally there is Scripture—infallible as always. Clearly this Temple will someday stand. Clearly it will be a Temple of God, in the ancient traditions of those consecrated houses that have graced this site in ages gone by.

What will happen?

It is the thesis of this book that the Tribulation Temple will be built; that it will stand on the site of the Dome of the Rock; that it will be a genuine Jerusalem Temple comparable to Solomon's and Herod's; that it will house sacrifice and oblations; that the Antichrist will cause these to cease in the Temple as prophesied; that it will be destroyed so that Christ may raise the final Temple—His house on the earth.

3

Opening Pandora's Box—
Prayer on the Mount

AS WE STATED in the introduction to this revised edition, it has been several years since *Satan in the Sanctuary* was first published. During that time some remarkable events have come to pass, further intensifying the imminency of Temple prophecy.

We expected that. If we are, in fact, approaching the biblical "end times," and if, as the Scriptures state, the Tribulation Temple is to be constructed in connection with that period, we ought to be seeing some progress. And, in fact, we are.

When *Satan in the Sanctuary* was written, Israel was very far removed from actual Temple-building plans. But, as this updated section will show, some very real developments toward the existence of the third Temple have now transpired. Truly this is the first time in modern history, since the destruction of the second Temple in A.D. 70, that we might well report the steps toward the rebuilding of the Temple of God.

The most striking of the new developments is the insistence of some Israelis to pray on the Temple Mount itself, rather than at the Western Wall below. Defying both traditional prohibitions against desecrating the site as well as public policy today, some devout Jews are pressing for the right to offer their prayers directly into God's ear, as it were, at the very site of the ancient sanctuary.

This would seem to be a logical first step toward Temple construction. A reasonable scenario might be the following: (1) prayer on the mount on an individual and unorganized basis; (2) organized prayer on the mount, supported by larger numbers of worshipers; (3) sacrificial worship on the mount; and finally, (4) the building of the Temple to house the worship.

But obviously this would be a difficult procedure to follow, with many pitfalls. Indeed, the very first step, the praying on the mount, has been met by outraged rebuffs from all sides. The rabbinic community, the Israeli establishment (who want to maintain a low profile about Temple Mount affairs in these times), and, predictably, the Muslims have all reacted with alarm. To the rabbis, Jewish prayer on the mount, which is not properly outfitted with the Temple, is invalid worship; to the Israeli secular establishment it amounts to a provocation of the Arabs; to the Muslims it represents encroachment of the most heinous kind, a usurping of an Islamic holy site.

The movement for communicating with God at His chosen place has not been very popular, to say the least. "There is no new thing under the sun" (Eccles 1:9).

A Momentous Decision

As it happened, a small prayer meeting in mid-1975 started a major Middle East crisis. A group of sincere but nonconforming Jewish worshipers elected to go up the hill to the summit of Mount Moriah and to pray virtually in the shadow of the Muslim holy places.

Those faithful who gathered to pray at the Western Wall

Opening Pandora's Box—Prayer on the Mount 41

that day must have been horrified to see the worshipers climb the hill and pass through the forbidden entrance to the upper level of the mount, where the Temples of Solomon and Herod stood. (Entrance to the mount proper is theoretically forbidden to all owing to the holiness of the place in Jewish law, and tourists are all handed an announcement to that effect when they pass through the gates at the top of the hill. But this prohibition, in the spirit of peacekeeping, is never enforced.)

If the Jews were horrified, the Muslims were utterly incensed by this intrusion. The Muslim Arab authorities on the mount considered the prayer a sacrilege to the Islamic worship in progress at the site. Jewish police summarily arrested the worshipers and the matter was considered closed, as the Muslims shuddered with indignation.

But that was not at all the end of the issue. Those arrested were due a trial, and several months later, in January 1976, they had their day in court. The defendants were determined to argue their right to the mount and they rose to the occasion regardless of the formidable opposition on all sides of the unique, emotional litigation. They simply stated that they had a right to the mount by all biblical and legal reckoning and they meant to exercise that right.

It was assumed that the prayer group would lose the case; there would be real trouble if they won.

But they did win, and there was real trouble!

In her decision, Israeli Magistrate Ruth Or found the worshipers not guilty and declared that Jews have a right to pray on the mount. Few judicial decisions could have created more shock waves in an area of constant and increasing bad will. Riots on the Temple Mount ensued at once, with the Muslims decrying the affront, and soon the entire West Bank of Israel was literally up in arms. The argument wound up in the United Nations, where it remained, for all practical purposes, disconcertingly unsolved.

The *Jerusalem Post* followed the entire saga of disagreement and protest very closely, running weekly articles. The reportage began with a story on the Arab rioting immediately following Magistrate Or's decision:

TEMPLE MOUNT PROTEST—8 HELD

JERUSALEM POST STAFF

Police on Sunday broke up a demonstration of some 500 East Jerusalem Arab high school pupils on the Temple Mount who were protesting against the acquittal of Jewish youth arrested nine months ago for praying on the sacred site.

A police spokesman said 12 demonstrators were arrested after the mob pelted security forces with stones, injuring one policeman.

The pupils gathered on the Temple Mount near the Al-Aksa mosque, shouting anti-Israel slogans and waving the flag of the Palestine Liberation Organization. A previous protest by 400 youths on Saturday ended peacefully.

The youths were protesting a decision two weeks ago by Magistrate's Court Judge Ruth Or that Jews have the right to pray on the Temple Mount, the site of the second Temple, destroyed by the Romans in 70 CE and now occupied by the Dome of the Rock and Al-Aksa (considered the third holiest site in Islam, after shrines in Mecca and Medina).

Police Minister Shlomo Hillel subsequently said that the ban on Jewish prayer on the Mount would continue, citing a Supreme Court decision of 1970.[1]

Indeed, the Israeli Supreme Court, in 1970, banned Jewish prayer on the mount, as the article alludes. This may have been done both in deference to *halacha,* the Jewish law, and to keep the peace. But the Supreme Court's decision had been tested before the inflammatory incident of 1975. In 1973, just previous to the Yom Kippur War, two Israeli citizens of note met for prayer on the mount on the holy day of *Tisha B'Av* (the Ninth of Av). The day was particularly appropriate for memorial prayers on the mount; on this "day of sorrow" both past Temples were destroyed. Something of a local debate ensued on that occasion, but nothing like the rioting that followed the 1976 decision. The *Post* reported:

POLICE BAN TESTED BY PRAYERS ON MT. MORIAH

JERUSALEM POST REPORTER

Jerusalem City Councillor Rabbi Louis Rabinowitz and Knesset Member Binyamin Halevi, a former Supreme Court Justice prayed and recited Lamentations for Tisha B'Av on the Temple Mount yesterday, despite police efforts to expel them.

Dr. Halevi went along with his Gahal colleague, who had been expelled from the Mount by police last year to help him force police to make a test case out of his pray-in.

Rabbi Rabinowitz and Dr. Halevi showed up at the Mount around 11 a.m. They sat on the steps not far from the western parapet overlooking the Western Wall, and began their recitation in low voices. They had not informed the press, or asked anyone to accompany them.

Dr. Halevi told *The Post* that after Moslem Council inspectors and Arab policemen informed them they were infringing the law, a Jewish police officer warned them they were praying in a place where the *halacha* prohibited prayer, and were also causing a potential disturbance. Dr. Halevi said the police officer tried to shut his *siddur* to prevent him praying, whereupon he told the officer that he was violating his Knesset immunity.

Rabbi Rabinowitz invited the officer to take his name and identity number and have him summoned as a lawbreaker. "This will be a test case," the rabbi told the officer. "The law may prohibit public prayer but I am praying privately and quietly, while it is the police who are causing a disturbance and making a crowd collect."

The police officer persuaded the two worshippers to move a little towards the Moors Gate, which gives access to the Western Wall. He took their particulars, shooed away a handful of curious onlookers, mostly Arab children, and kept close watch on them till they finished their prayers and left.

Rabbi Rabinowitz told *The Post* that as far as he was concerned, the *halacha* did not forbid him praying on that part of the Temple Mount.[2]

Rabbi Rabinowitz's view of the *halacha* and Jewish rights to the mount may well have been what prompted the more massive prayer movement in 1975, with its accompanying repercussions. Certainly the Supreme Court would not have spoken on the question at all if it had not foreseen such incidents.

JEWISH AND CHRISTIAN CONCERN

For the Muslims to express strenuous objection to Jewish prayer on the mount, and even to riot, is rather to be expected. But there was also a great deal of Jewish and Christian concern over the incident of 1975. Letters poured in to the *Post,* mostly expressing the obvious point that the mount is, after all, a Jewish prayer ground. We submit the following letters as representative of the Jewish and Christian views:

LETTERS

PRAYERS ON THE TEMPLE MOUNT

To the Editor of The Jerusalem Post

Sir,—Apparently, few people were aware that, since June 1967, Jews had no right to pray on the Temple Mount because of the strong objections of the local Islamic authorities. Thanks to a courageous judge in Jerusalem, Mrs. Ruth Or, this amazing situation will now be corrected. Such a situation should never have been tolerated, but is just another example of the strange lack of dignity in the official Israeli approach to other religions.

While on the subject of the Temple Mount, may I draw your your attention to the fact that the Islamic authorities have transformed the inside of the marvellous Golden Gate into the junkyard of the two Mosques, and its direct approach is barred by barbed wire. The Golden Gate is the site of a former Christian basilica and the gate through which the Jews expect the Messiah to arrive and the Christians expect the second coming of Jesus. Such desecration should be stopped immediately and, once cleaned up, the site could serve for concerts of spiritual music and ecumenical gatherings.

REV. CLAUDE DUVERNOY,
DIRECTOR
Christian Action for Israel
Jerusalem, February 6.[3]

READERS' LETTERS

TEMPLE MOUNT IS JEWISH

To the Editor of The Jerusalem Post

Sir,—The Israel correspondent of the CBS on the Voice of America (March 15) informed us that current Arab disturbances in certain towns of the "occupied West Bank" were sparked off by a recent court decision upholding Jewish rights of prayer at the Temple Mount, the "site of the famed el Aksa Mosque"—and here comes the gem—"also" regarded as holy ground by the Jews.

Whether facetious, malicious or plain ignorant, such reference to the Temple Mount obscures the fact that the two Jewish Temples stood here for close to a millennium, until finally razed to the ground by the Romans in 70 C.E. During that period, it was the hub of Jewish existence, temporal as well as spiritual. The two Moslem structures, an afterthought of the 7th century C.E., were built there precisely because of the Temple Mount's paramount sanctity in Judaism. Even so, the site comes a poor third to Mecca and Medina, the twin cynosures of Islam.

Unfortunately, Israel Government moves, such as the appeal against the above mentioned court decision, only add to the existing confusion. No less perplexing is the Israel Rabbinate's official insistence on the inadmissibility of steps calculated to reassert Jewish presence on any part of the Temple Mount, when the very act of regaining it is known to supersede the ritual prohibition. As a result we have the tragi-comic situation of an Israeli constabulary "protecting" the actual heart of the Jewish title to this country as a de facto Moslem site, against would-be Jewish "intruders."

AVNER TOMASCHOFF[4]
Jerusalem.

A substantial number of both Jews and Christians were in favor of Jewish prayer on the mount, which is certainly biblical, if not very diplomatic in these tense times.

46 *Israel and Tomorrow's Temple*

The Jewish writer above saw the obvious irony in the situation at the mount, where Jewish police keep Jews off the supposed Muslim site. It was "tragi-comic" to him, as it would be, we suppose, to King Solomon. The Christian correspondent looked to the East Gate, where prophecy states that Jesus will return to Jerusalem, and deplored the Arab desecration there. His grief was genuine.

Dry Bones [5]

A GROUP OF JEWISH "NATIONALISTS" TRIED TO "PRAY" ON THE TEMPLE MOUNT..

..SETTING OFF RIOTS AND DEMONSTRATIONS THAT HAVE RUPTURED THE PEACE WITH..

..A NOISE ECHOING AROUND THE WORLD..

I WONDER WHAT THEY WERE PLANNING TO PRAY FOR?

©1976 Kirschen

Opening Pandora's Box—Prayer on the Mount

Obviously, the Temple Mount, the holy site of the biblical Jews, is a shrine to both Judaism and Christianity, and there is no sign that its significance will decrease in the future. We can probably expect ongoing approaches by the Jews, in spite of Muslim resistance, in keeping with the program for the building of the Tribulation Temple.

In fact, in early March 1976, another, much more organized attempt to pray on the mount ensued, and this time there was a public debate on the scene. The police maintained a low profile as this modern version of the rivalry of Isaac and Ishmael unfolded. The *Post* reported at length:

NATIONAL NEWS

POLICE BLOCK JEWISH BID TO PRAY ON TEMPLE MOUNT

By ABRAHAM RABINOVICH

Jerusalem Post Reporter

The first organized attempt by Jewish nationalists to pray on the Temple Mount since a magistrates court ruling last January permitting such prayer was turned back by police Sunday.

Some 50 blue-uniformed Betar youth led by two Likud city councilmen—Rabbi L. I. Rabinowitz and Gershon Solomon—were halted just outside the Mograbi Gate, on the ramp leading up from the Western Wall, by Jerusalem Police Chief David Kraus. He was backed by a line of blue-uniformed police firmly blocking the entrance.

When Solomon announced the group's intention of entering the Temple Mount to pray, Kraus said: "Since there is reason to believe that your entering the Temple Mount and praying there will lead to a disturbance of the peace, we forbid you to enter."

Solomon accused Kraus of holding in contempt the ruling by Magistrate Ruth Or on January 28 that Jews had the right to pray on the Mount. "The ruling," said Solomon, "explicitly states that banning of Jews from praying on the Temple Mount is a violation of the law."

Kraus said he was not holding any court ruling in contempt. "As commander of police in Jerusalem, I have reason to believe that this would cause a public disturbance. I will do everything to prevent the peace from being disturbed."

Police Minister Shlomo Hillel, in ordering the police to prevent Jewish prayer on the Temple Mount, cited a Supreme Court decision of 1970 that, while Jews had the right to pray there, the authorities had the right to withhold that right if its exercise would lead to a public disturbance.

Solomon said there was no other place in the world where Jews were prevented from praying in a place holy to them.

"We haven't come to demonstrate, only to pray quietly. I don't think that praying in our most holy place is a disturbance of the peace."

When one of the Betar leaders asked whether the police were unable to preserve the peace if Jews prayed on the Temple Mount, Kraus said, "At this stage, no."

After an exchange that lasted five minutes, Rabbi Rabinowitz led the group in the *minha* prayer, after which they peacefully dispersed.

While this confrontation was going on, close to 100 Arab youths were milling about on the Temple Mount outside Al-Aksa Mosque, where a smaller number of adult Moslems were waiting for the beginning of the evening prayer.

Inside Mograbi Gate were a small number of police with shields, helmets and batons. However, the police maintained a decidedly low profile on both sides of the gate, both in numbers and deportment; and their defusing efforts were successful.

Only an occasional Arab policeman casually patrolled around the Temple Mount, the rest of the police keeping their positions at the gate. Tourists who continued to visit the mosques during the incident sensed the tension in the air but did not know what was happening.

At a press conference afterwards, Solomon said attempts would be made now on a daily basis to pray on the Temple Mount. Kraus told reporters that the ban on Jewish prayer there would continue to be enforced.

Betar, the Revisionist-Herut youth movement, has a nationalist rather than religious orientation; and many of the participants in Sunday's attempted pray-in wore the paper skullcaps issued at the Western Wall rather than headcover of their own. Before they mounted the ramp to Mograbi Gate they were harangued by a black-garbed Orthodox Jew, who accused them of violating religious law by entering the Temple Mount.[6]

Finally, on March 23, 1976, the *Post* editorialized a very thought-provoking opinion: Judge Or had opened "Pandora's Box." There was going to be some real trouble over the Temple site:

NATIONAL NEWS

PANDORA'S BOX ON TEMPLE MOUNT

Magistrate Ruth Or's ruling that Jews had the right to pray on the Temple Mount—and that the Israeli authorities should draw up regulations allowing them to do so—has opened up a Pandora's box of complications, writes Post Reporter Abraham Rabinovich.

IT WAS A DECISION by a freshman judge in the lowest court in the land in a routine case, or so it seemed.

In its wake, during the past seven weeks, there have come riots in towns throughout the West Bank, shopkeepers' strikes, school shutdowns, hundreds of arrests, the resignation of five West Bank municipal councils, cries of outrage from Islamic nations, and a pledge by the UN Secretary General that he would take up the matter.

Magistrate Ruth Or did not content herself with acquitting the eight Jewish youths accused of disturbing the peace by praying on the Temple Mount.

The eight were innocent, she explained, because they had the right as Jews to pray at Judaism's most sacred site. She chastised the authorities for attempting to prevent such prayer, and called upon the Ministry for Religious Affairs to draw up regulations spelling out when and where Jews might pray on the Temple Mount.

In this seemingly inadvertent fashion was raised an issue full of religious passions, and one that has remained dormant through the decades of confrontation between the two peoples.

It remained dormant for two reasons that are now being challenged as a result of Judge Or's ruling, one religious and the other political.

The ban upon entry to the Temple Mount issued by the Rabbinical Council following the Six-Day War—and still posted outside Mograbi Gate—reflected an attitude dating from Maimonides in the 12th century. Maimonides maintained that because of the uncertainty as to the location of the Holy of Holies—

entry to which was restricted, on pain of death, to the High Priest on Yom Kippur—Jews should stay off the Mount altogether.

The renowned philanthropist, Sir Moses Montefiore, was threatened with excommunication when he visited the Temple Mount, not being aware of the prohibition. The ban has been strongly upheld in recent generations by the rabbis of Jerusalem and is by far the dominant religious attitude today.

Nevertheless, the ban has been challenged from time to time over the centuries, most recently by Rabbi Shlomo Goren, who declared after the Six-Day War, when he was Chief Military Chaplain to the Armed Forces, that there were places on the Temple Mount clearly outside the area occupied by the Temple and therefore open to Jews and Jewish prayer.

LAST WEEK, Religious Affairs Minister Yitzhak Raphael, mindful of Judge Or's recommendation that regulations be drawn up for Jewish prayer on the Temple Mount, asked the two Chief Rabbis for their opinion. Sephardi Chief Rabbi Ovadia Yosef responded immediately that the ban on Jews entering the Temple Mount was still in force. Ashkenazi Chief Rabbi Shlomo Goren has not yet replied. If he advocates revocation of the ban, the question would presumably go to the 12-man Supreme Rabbinical Council.

The secular authorities, unlike the religious, have permitted Jews to enter the Temple Mount, even taking over control of the Mograbi Gate in 1967 at Defence Minister Moshe Dayan's order to ensure free access during hours when they would not interfere with Moslem prayer. The authorities, however, have consistently refused to permit Jews to pray on the mount, since this might be a provocation to the Moslems.

Periodic attempts over the past few years by nationalist Jewish youths and others to pray here have been broken up. In 1970 a five-judge panel of the Supreme Court ruled that while Jews had the inherent right to pray on the Temple Mount the government could refuse to permit such prayer if it might lead to a disturbance of the peace. Judge Or's ruling is now being appealed by the State Attorney, and it will, in all likelihood work its way up to the Supreme Court.

The drive for Jewish prayer on the Temple Mount is being led by two Likud members of the Jerusalem City Council, Gershon Solomon and Rabbi L. I. Rabinowitz. They are acting without the support of their own party—indeed, against the opposition of key Likud leaders who object to Jewish prayer on the Temple Mount because of its political explosiveness. If such strong objections are to be found in the principal nationalist party, which itself represents only a minority of the electorate, it is safe to assume that the great majority of the population is at least as opposed. Gush Emunim, which has not hesitated to challenge the Government head-on in asserting its views of Jewish rights of settlement in the Holy Land, has refrained — apparently on religious grounds — from walking through the door to the Temple Mount that Judge Or tried to open.

The chief vehicle for pressing the drive, such as it is, for Jewish prayer on the Temple Mount has been the Betar Youth Movement, which is a nationalist and not a religious organisation. By doing so they are admittedly challenging an area of ambiguity. The Protection of Holy Places Law permits "access to the different religions to the places sacred to them." The Israeli Government would be the last body in the world to deny that the Temple Mount is sacred to the Jews, and it does permit access, yet it will not permit the Jews to pray there.

By their insistence on Jewish prayer on the Temple Mount, Solomon and his colleagues— who have rarely mustered as many as a dozen adults at any of their pray-in attempts—are opening the way, theoretically at least, to demands by Moslems or Christians to pray at the Western Wall if they feel it is holy to them.

The present situation is indeed ambiguous, but it is ambiguities that often permit nations, like individuals, to go on living together.[7]

It is hard to imagine a prayer meeting giving rise to international concern anywhere else in the world. The Temple site at Mount Moriah has become a center of global controversy, as, in fact, it always was. Where the past controversies were spiritual in nature, we now see the secular world deeply involved; where the question used to be, Shall we Jews offer our sacrifices here, Lord? it has now become, Will this Middle Eastern rioting and United Nations debating take us into World War III?

How typical that God's choice of place, that thirty-four acre site, is so important in the affairs of men. Indeed, this place at the center of the earth is still very crucial.

It is likely that the Arabs' rioting represents a Muslim point of view that the Jews are seriously trying to take over the site and rebuild the Temple of God. They recognize that prayer on the mount is a first step toward rebuilding, and they are determined to dig in at this point and stop the progress. They may feel that the movement toward Jewish control of the mount will be irreversible if worshipers are permitted there, and they may well be right.

To be sure, the Jews have not approached the mount in great numbers, but they have been represented by influential citizens. The Jerusalem city councilmen probably give the Muslims more pause than the rabbis and their followers, but any Jews on the mount worry them.

On Sunday, March 21, 1976, the Israeli Supreme Court felt obliged to reassert its original position on Jewish prayer on the mount. It reaffirmed that, while Jews have a right to pray on the mount, the Israeli police may forbid such prayer in order to maintain the peace. The court was both sympathetic to the aspirations of the devout worshipers, and realistic about the social and political implications in the situation.

The Jerusalem Bureau of the Associated Press circulated internationally this newest development, and people everywhere read, "The Israeli Supreme Court Sunday supported a government ban on Jewish prayers on the Temple Mount, the disputed Jerusalem holy site that has touched off the worst wave of anti-Israeli rioting in occupied Jordan in nine years."[8] The article also reported on the activities of firebrand Rabbi Moshe Levinger, leader of fourteen hundred Jews living near Hebron, the site of major riots. Rabbi Levinger and his followers were furious with the Arab demonstrators and thought that the Israeli army, called in to quiet the rioting, had dealt too leniently with the foe. The

Opening Pandora's Box—Prayer on the Mount 53

rabbi's forces were armed. The Arab mayor of Hebron resigned, becoming the eighth West Bank leader to resign in protest of the disturbing situation, Associated Press reported.

In the United States, the office of the Consulate General of Israel in Houston endeavored to explain the decision of the Supreme Court. A "Policy Background" statement distributed by the Consulate General on March 25, 1976, confirmed that " the right of a Jew—as that of a Moslem—to pray on the Temple Mount is fundamental and unquestionable," but that "In the matter of Jewish prayers on the Temple Mount, the Government has deliberately and voluntarily relinquished a clear right for the sake of communal harmony."

The *Jerusalem Post,* certainly a free press if there ever was one, continued to take issue with the Supreme Court's position, however. On March 30 that paper published an article stating that the court was ignoring the central issue—"the magistrate's ruling that the Jews have the right to pray on the Temple Mount and that the Ministry for Religious Affairs should draw up regulations permitting such prayer."

But clearly, as long as the police forbid Jewish prayer on the mount, feeling that it will lead to a serious disturbance of the peace, and as long as the Supreme Court backs up the police, the matter is at a standstill. As matters stand, only Jewish outlaws pray on the mount.

An attempt at a middle-ground prayer effort was made by a group who searched the mount and the law, and chose a spot which they felt was definitely away from the prohibited areas. The mount is spacious, after all, and one might find places away from the mosques and away from the site of the ancient Holy of Holies that would not bring on a confrontation with either the Arabs or the rabbis. The group also made sure that their prayers did not coincide with Muslim prayer calls, which occur five times each day. The leader of the group, Louis Rabinowitz, wrote to the *Post* with searching questions:

> Is it really hot-headed fanaticism to hope that permission may be granted to Jews to pray at a time when Moslem prayer is not taking place, and at a spot far removed both from the site of their devotions and from the area prohibited by those who maintain that such a prohibition exists? And do those who oppose the plea really believe that a ban on prayer by Jews at the site most sacred to them will bring Arab agitation to an end?[9]

Rabinowitz is still in conflict with the letter of the Supreme Court's ruling, of course, but his action to find a way despite all opposition is representative of the strength of the Jewish desire to pray on the mount. With all of the troubles with the Arabs, and with all of the peacemaking attempts of the Supreme Court, the Jews still want to go to God "upon one of the mountains which I will tell thee of" (Gen 22:2). Since Genesis 22, the chosen people have sought God at the place He directed Abraham, and by all spiritual reckoning, this is their right.

And the contention? The troubles with the Arabs—and with the whole world, for that matter?

Well, when has God's plan been easily fulfilled? When has prophecy happened by the agreed-upon will of men? Shall we expect this nearly final preparation of the Tribulation, the rebuilding of the Temple of God, to be easy?

When God's plans progress the world trembles, and it has ever been so. Armies have marched, empires fallen, kings have been deposed, and legions of human beings have contested in bloody battles the progress of God's plan for men.

Opening Pandora's Box—Prayer on the Mount

But God's plans go on, all the same. The Temple of God in Jerusalem will soon be rebuilt, despite all furor to the contrary, and we who wait and watch prophecies develop according to the certain guarantee of the Word of God, can only anticipate eagerly the further developments from the Holy City.

4

The Jerusalem Great Synagogue— A Halfway House?

WHEN THE JEWS began to build the Jerusalem Great Synagogue in 1974, many prophecy watchers felt, "This is it! Here comes the Tribulation Temple!"

Indeed, some teachers of prophecy still hold that the magnificent new synagogue under construction in the Holy City is sufficient fulfillment of the third-Temple prophecies; but the synagogue instead represents a compromise plan, something at which the chosen people have always been good. The synagogue is not the third Temple, but it is a wonderful synagogue!

The Jerusalem Great Synagogue is the result of the frustration apparent in the idea of rebuilding the true Temple of God on its appropriate site. If the Temple in all its glory cannot be had at this time, then at least the chosen people may have a common place to worship, close to the Temple site in Jerusalem and serving as a central meeting place of worship for all Jews of the world.

Dr. Maurice Jaffe, president of the Union of Israel Synagogues and chairman of the building committee for the Jerusalem Great Synagogue, concedes, "We're not prepared for it [the actual Temple of God] spiritually, politically or morally," but the synagogue is another matter entirely. Dr. Jaffe is very realistic about the Temple obstacles—"The last thing we want to do is go knocking down mosques"—but he is extremely enthusiastic about the synagogue: "We are doing everything possible to make this the most beautiful Synagogue in the world, for Jerusalem deserves nothing less."[1]

There was confusion when the first announcements about the synagogue came out; a reporter utilized the term *temple* in describing the proposed structure. An Associated Press release ran under the headline "Second Coming Linked to New Jewish Temple," and of course it raised quite a stir. However, the term *Temple* is used commonly throughout Reform Judaism today to refer simply to a house of worship. Dr. Jaffe stressed the similarities and the differences between the Great Synagogue and a rebuilt Temple of God in a July 1974 interview with Associated Press writer George Cornell:

SECOND COMING LINKED TO NEW JEWISH TEMPLE

By GEORGE W. CORNELL

NEW YORK (AP)—An aura of mystery surrounds the idea of restoring the Jewish Temple in Jerusalem. Both for many Christians and Jews, it's a longed-for dream, a Messianic sign. It is not yet. But something like it is happening.

Construction is due to begin on the first large, central Jewish house of worship in the Holy City since the destruction of the Temple 1,904 years ago.

"NO ONE IS SUGGESTING that this means the restoration of the Temple," says Rabbi Dr. Maurice A. Jaffee, president of the Union of Israel Synagogues which is sponsoring the project. "But there are parallels."

For one thing, the prospective new "Jerusalem Great Synagogue" is planned as a central, representative sanctuary to which Jewish pilgrims from all over the world may come to pray—just as they did in the Temple of old.

In another respect, every Jew everywhere is being encouraged to contribute something to the building of the new edifice, even if it amounts to no more than a half shekel—the basic tribute of each practicing Jew to the ancient Temple.

Furthermore, the new house of worship is being built of a special radiant stone like that of the Temple of Bible times, and is to be situated next to the headquarters of Israel's rabbinic authority, as was the historic Temple.

"THERE ARE MANY analogies, but we're wary of drawing comparisons," Dr. Jaffee said in an interview. "One gets in hot water even to hint at such a thing. Conditions are out of the question for re-establishing the Temple."

Doing so, to many Christians who interpret the Bible literally, would be a prophetic indication of the imminent return of Christ. Many Jews also link restoration of the Temple to a coming Messiah.[2]

The latent longing for the golden days of biblical Israel is apparent through the rabbi's remarks. Dr. Jaffee, along with every other religious Jew everywhere, would rather have the holy shrine of the Temple of God in Jerusalem than the Great Synagogue, even with all its beauty and significance. But perhaps the synagogue will accomplish the purpose of bringing world Jewry to Jerusalem more often, as in the days when the grand festivals drew the chosen people together in common worship. Perhaps Jews of many lands will regard the synagogue as next to the Temple in godliness and significance.

And again, we have a step toward the Temple. As with the steadily increasing pressure for prayer on the mount, the Synagogue represents a move toward rebuilding the Temple of God. If world Jewry recovers its pilgrim ways of old and comes to the Great Synagogue to worship, or even if the Jews of foreign lands merely agree to support the synagogue project financially, we have a real identification with a "central shrine" of Judaism. Once the concept is understood by Jews everywhere, rebuilding the Temple becomes a more understandable and realistic matter. Should the obstacles in some way diminish, the Jews will be ready.

Not only Jews of the world but also Christians are invited to take part in the building of the Great Jerusalem Synagogue. Contributions are accepted, and Christians are extended an invitation to inspect the construction site of the progressing synagogue. The senior author wrote an inquiry to Dr. Jaffee and received the following gracious reply:

8th Nissan, 5736
8th April, 1976

Reverend Thomas McCall,
5324 West N.W. Highway,
Dallas, Texas 75220,
U.S.A.

My dear Reverend McCall,

Your letter of the 28th January eventually reached us and I must apologise for our delay.

It was indeed kind of you to make inquiries about the Jerusalem Great Synagogue. For your information I am sending you herewith a pamphlet on the subject. The exterior of the building has been extremely improved since the pamphlet has published but generally we are doing everything possible to make this the most beautiful Synagogue in the world for Jerusalem deserves nothing less. Cheques can be sent to our New York office, the address being the Jerusalem Great Synagogue, Suite 1500, 2 Penn Plaza, New York 1001. Where the donor wishes to benefit from the tax-free excemption the cheques should be made payable to the American Hechal Shlomo Committee Inc.

We are looking forward to hearing from you and hope

that we might have the opportunity of receiving you in Holy Jerusalem and showing you the construction site.

With kindest regards and best wishes.

> Yours sincerely,
> Maurice A. Jaffe,
> Chairman.

Thus, the world, not just the Jews, is invited to take part in this glorious work, the building of what we might call a "halfway house" toward the Temple of God. The people of Israel realize that Christians have a great interest in the progress of the Temple rebuilding program, however hesitating and difficult that progress might be, and they appreciate Christian concern for the Jews. The burden of financing such a work is heavy, of course, and there is precedent for outside help. We saw in the thrilling story of King David that Araunah the Jebusite graciously provided his valuable land for the sovereign's building plans toward the first Temple of God. May the believing non-Jews of today see the value and sanctity of this work as clearly as Araunah did. Even though Israel will build the Temple while not yet believing in Christ, and even though the Tribulation Temple will be desecrated by the Antichrist, Christians can rejoice in all steps leading toward the third Temple as the fulfillment of Bible prophecy and affirmation of the nearness of the second coming of Christ.

The Foundation Stone

The idea of the Great Jerusalem Synagogue did not originate in the present generation. As long ago as forty years, rabbinical leaders in Israel urged such a project. A brochure published by the Committee for the Erection of the Jerusalem Great Synagogue presents the words of Rabbis HaCohen

The Jerusalem Great Synagogue—A Halfway House?

Kook and Jacob Meir, chief rabbis of the Holy Land in the 1930s:

> How is it even possible to imagine the large Jewish Community in the new Jerusalem—which is, after all, the main and largest part of the City—without a central synagogue which one can aptly call the Great Central Synagogue of Jerusalem?
>
> How is it possible even to give expression to the strange but nevertheless true statement that "Jerusalem the Great and Holy" has no large, central synagogue?[3]

Thus, even before Israel became a state as we know it now, and even before the old and new Jerusalems were merged into one city, the desire for the Great Synagogue existed. But the dream awaited the 1967 Six-Day War, when the Jews were able to repossess the Old City, containing the ancient Jewish quarter and the Temple Mount.

The foundation stone of the new Great Synagogue was actually laid in June 1969, though few people in the world then knew it. Considerable ceremony was undertaken with the laying of the foundation, which was observed by Israeli government religious and lay dignitaries. The brochure goes on:

> On the 8th of Tamuz, 5729 (June 24, 1969 A.D.) the Ceremony of the laying of the Foundation Stone of the Jerusalem Great Synagogue took place in United Jerusalem, the capital city of the independent State of Israel, in the presence of the President of the State, the Chief Rabbis of Israel, Cabinet Ministers, Members of the Diplomatic and Consular Corps, the Mayor of the city and chief rabbis and distinguished lay leaders of Communities in Israel and throughout the Diaspora.[4]

The presence of such varied representation of the state and the Jewish people certainly shows the uniformity of the desire for a major Jerusalem house of worship—the first in over nineteen hundred years. And the speed with which the project was undertaken, just two years after the war, rather shows the eagerness of the faithful.

Why A "Great Synagogue"?

The purposes and nature of the Great Synagogue are explained by the same official brochure. The project is mainly to fill a glaring deficiency.

The Jerusalem Great Synagogue is to be unique among the synagogues of the world, in its setting, its sanctity, and its magnificence. It is intended to be as beautiful as its sacred purposes deserve, and truly, it will be one of the most important Jewish structures in the world.

The sponsors of the project deplore the fact that in Jerusalem, the holiest of all cities and the capital of the State of Israel, there stands no large, representative synagogue. The Gentile capitals of the world enjoy what Jerusalem lacks, and the Great Synagogue will repair this deficiency. It goes without saying that the synagogue is needed in Jerusalem.

King Solomon himself would be impressed with the care and effort to be expended on making this synagogue a monumental masterpiece of design and construction. Its interior decoration will leave worshipers weak with admiration, if the directors of the project have their way. A wonder of the modern world is under construction in Israel. The synagogue is being planned to surpass in beauty all of its forerunners and contemporaries, and to become the central shrine of Judaism and the world.

It takes a lot of help and a lot of work. The directors have appealed to Jews and interested non-Jews throughout the

The Jerusalem Great Synagogue—A Halfway House? 63

world in this effort, stressing to those of Europe who lost so many synagogues in the holocaust that this is the way to rebuild. They ask that this edifice not be the result of the generosity of a few, but rather the heartfelt donation of the Jewish people of the world to "those who dwell in Zion."

STONES OF GOLD

The Great Synagogue will accommodate large crowds but at the same time not sacrifice "the spirit of intimacy and warmth which has always characterized the Divine services in Jerusalem," according to the brochure. The sanctuary will seat between six and seven hundred in the winter off-season, when tourism drops, but can be expanded to accommodate fifteen hundred during the High Holy Days of the other seasons. Women will be seated in a low balcony with a clear view of the proceedings, according to the Orthodox tradition. The acoustics of the auditorium will be of such excellent nature that no electronic sound system will be necessary in the building.

The committee has provided that all services will be conducted in accordance with strict Orthodox rites, with dignity and decorum befitting the setting and tradition. The finest cantor (or "chanter" of prayers) and choir will be available at all times. (Sacrificial worship, of course, would not be included in the Orthodox rites in the Great Synagogue. As we have seen, God provided for sacrifices only on the Temple Mount itself.)

It should be appreciated that this beautiful building will be very costly for Israel. Each single stone in the massive edifice is said to cost one hundred dollars, and the interior furniture and appointments will come to over two million dollars! It is probable that the Great Jerusalem Synagogue will truly surpass the grandeur of all synagogues of the world.

The costly exterior stones are very special. Anyone who has ever been to Israel can testify of the remarkable character of the Jerusalem stone, seemingly designed by God Himself for a unique effect on the eye. As the brochure specifies:

> The Jerusalem Great Synagogue will be built from that beautiful Jerusalem stone which is known to change its colour throughout the day, the sun giving it a golden tinge towards evening—hence the expression, "Jerusalem, the Golden."[5]

Like Solomon's Temple, the Great Synagogue will have a tall tower in front, divided to represent the two tablets of stone bearing the Ten Commandments. The interior architecture will reflect the two major branches of the Jewish people today, the Sephardic (Oriental) and the Ashkenazic (European), along with a blending of unique features of Jerusalem.

The choir will sing from a sunken area, to be heard clearly but not to be seen. The roof above the choir platform will be convertible—able to be opened to the sky—in order to accommodate the Jewish wedding custom of marrying "directly under the sky."

Twelve stained-glass windows will surround the sanctuary, and a specially designed window more than twenty meters high (over sixty feet) will divide the tablets forming the central tower and face the Old City and the Temple site. Thus, as do all synagogues throughout the world, the Great Synagogue will proclaim its subservience to the holy Mount Moriah, site of the ancient Temples of God.

THE SYNAGOGUE AND THE TEMPLE

With all of its planned magnificence, it is no wonder that the Great Synagogue has the occasional honor of being

The Jerusalem Great Synagogue—A Halfway House?

called the Temple of God for this time. But, as we have said, this synagogue is not the Tribulation Temple.

The true Temple, when it is built, will dwarf this beautiful synagogue and make it fade into insignificance.

We can reason that if the Jewish people would spend such effort and such burdensome amounts of money on a central synagogue, they will do even more for the Temple. We have seen throughout this history of the Temples of God what sacrifices the chosen people were willing to make in past times for the true Temples. We have gone into much detail about the Jerusalem Great Synagogue to show that they have not lost their zeal for serving God in this way.

Is the synagogue a step toward the rebuilding of the Temple of God on its proper site? We think that it is. We think it establishes important precedents toward the Temple rebuilding; it focuses world Jewish attention on Jerusalem; it creates a central shrine for Jewish worship; it adorns Jerusalem, God's holy city.

And, most importantly, it makes the chosen people yearn for the real thing!

5

Step by Step—A Plan of Action

AS WE HAVE GATHERED from the biblical experiences of Israel, not just anybody can build the Temple of God.

Almost all religious Jews want the Temple to be rebuilt, eventually, and this important matter has been in their prayers since the Herodian Temple was destroyed in A.D. 70. There is certainly little question of *whether* the Temple should be rebuilt, but rather *when* and, most importantly, by *whom?*

Building the Temple has always been considered a most sacred project, to be undertaken only after the deepest consideration of the will of God. We recall that when God commissioned the building of the first Temple He did not permit so celebrated and successful a King of Israel as David to proceed with the actual work. "Thou hast shed blood abundantly," God pointed out to the disappointed monarch, "and hast made great wars: thou shalt not build a house unto my name" (1 Chron 22:8).

The task passed instead to Solomon, a "man of peace" and a more fitting builder of God's house on earth.

The second Temple was accomplished in the most difficult of times, only by those of pioneer spirit, willing to reclaim the ruins of Jerusalem and build while wielding a sword in defense of the site. God blessed their smaller work, and later it was enhanced to its fitting proportions and beauty. Again, only the consecrated participated in the building.

So, who shall undertake to build the third Temple of God? Who shall be considered fit to do this most sacred work? Who, then, is worthy?

We can see that even if the mount were clear and there were no international tensions involved with the rebuilding, the Jews would still hesitate before undertaking so monumental a task. How shall it be accomplished, and who will be called to do this?

Thus Saith The Lord

It may surprise people who do not appreciate the depth of faith to be found among the religious Israeli Jews that the rabbis look mainly to supernatural solutions to this problem. They hold various views about how the Temple may be rebuilt, assuming the site to be clear and the tensions relaxed, but all of their views reflect a serious consideration of God and the Messiah. They give the work its fitting respect.

The majority view is that it would be blasphemy for ordinary Jews simply to rebuild the Temple as they would any other structure. Instead, God Himself should reconsecrate the work, or provide the Messiah or a great prophet to undertake it.

Rabbi Mordechai HaCohen, a Jerusalem-born scholar and the author of various books on rabbinics, Jewish history, and the holy places, has gathered together the major views on the coming of the third Temple. He finds seven different positions on this question:

1. God will send down a perfect Temple of Fire from heaven, which, since it is built by God, will endure forever.
2. The Messiah will come and miraculously rebuild the Temple.
3. A non-miraculous king of Israel will demonstrate that

he is the Messiah by his devotion to the Law, by successfully rebuilding the Temple, and by successfully regathering the exiles to Israel.

4. Israel must first renew the sacrifices on the Temple Mount, and this will hasten the coming of the Messiah, who will then rebuild the Temple.
5. A divinely inspired Prophet of God must first reveal to the people the criteria needed to permit the rebuilding of the Temple and the sacrifices, but this cannot be accomplished until peace prevails and the majority of world Jewry dwells permanently in Israel.
6. Reconstruction of the Temple and resumption of the sacrifices should be undertaken by the common people in the immediate future, before the coming of the Messiah. The work should be guided by Jewish religious and historical sources, in four steps:
    A. Sacrifices offered on the site of the ancient altar
    B. Temple to be rebuilt to the specifications of Ezekiel 40-48
    C. Appearance of the Messiah to correct and embellish the structure and give further instruction on the sacrifices
    D. A lowering by the Almighty of the celestial Temple of Fire to stand within the manmade Temple.
7. Prayer services should be held on the Temple Mount in hopes that this will encourage world peace and hasten the redemption of Israel and mankind, as predicted in Isaiah 56:7.[1]

Rabbi HaCohen says that the "distinct minority" who hold the sixth view above "believe that prayer services should be organized on the site of the Temple." But he concedes, "Although there are Jews who favor the rebuilding of the

Temple and the resumption of the sacrifices at once, that is not likely to be the course of any Jewish action in the foreseeable future."[2]

Indeed, the latter view runs head-on into devastating political and religious consequences, as we have seen. If the Muslims take offense at the quiet prayer of small groups in nonsensitive places on the mount, we can imagine their response to animal sacrifices taking place at the very site of the ancient altar (directly beneath the Dome of the Rock). And of course, to build the Temple to Ezekiel's specifications at this time, which involves clearing the site, might well bring on something like World War III.

A Plan Of Action

Still, there are some Jews going right ahead, as well as they can, with plans for the rebuilding. They believe that it is an achievable goal, and with careful consideration for the worldly realities of the problem, they are making plans for action.

To be sure, these groups do not make a great deal of noise about their goal. Pressure is so strong in the Temple situation that those Jews who want to approach the rebuilding have great difficulty even expressing their views.

However, the authors located one such group in the United States who have designed jewelry for the women to wear to Temple worship and have composed music for the services! The group is called The Institute for Bible Design and is located in the New York area. In the May 14, 1974, issue of the *Jerusalem Post* the Institute ran a half-page advertisement with the following headline: MAY IT BE THY WILL O LORD OUR G-D THAT OUR HOLY TEMPLE BE REBUILT IN JERUSALEM IN OUR DAYS.

"MAY IT BE THY WILL O LORD OUR G-D THAT OUR HOLY TEMPLE BE REBUILT IN JERUSALEM" IN OUR DAYS

From our daily prayers.

We have dedicated the INSTITUTE OF BIBLE DESIGN to this purpose. Our object is to explore JEWISH sources to develop moral, political and social pressures with the ultimate object of rebuilding the TEMPLE.

A new learning experience is needed to bring world pressures into thinking about the TEMPLE. Through this experience, a new world of creativity in dress, conversation, dance, music and art will be developed. For example:

PIRKE AVOT 2:1

Know that above you is a Seeing eye, a hearing ear, And your deeds are written In a book.

ISAIAH 9:1

The people that walked In darkness have seen A great light.

PSALM 48:13-14

Walk about Zion; go around Her;.... That ye may tell it to the following generation.

If you are interested, you may join us by forwarding $25.00 to the INSTITUTE OF BIBLE DESIGN, P.O. Box 85, Fresh Meadows Station, Flushing, New York 11365 with your comments, and you will receive our first publication entitled:

"ON THE STUDY OF THE BIBLE WITHOUT THE BOOK"

TUESDAY, MAY 14, 1974 — THE JERUSALEM POST WEEKLY — PAGE THIRTEEN

Step by Step—A Plan of Action

(They write "G-D" in respect to the Jewish commandments concerning the unpronounceable name of the Lord. Actually writing out "GOD" is contrary to Orthodox practices).

The ad goes on to inform the Israeli public, "Our object is to explore JEWISH sources to develop moral, political and social pressures with the ultimate goal of rebuilding the TEMPLE." A complete copy of the ad, with its remarkable illustrations, follows:

The authors followed up on the offer in the ad and received the 142-page *On the Study of the Bible without the Book*. Most of this book is devoted to presenting the organization's unique, biblically oriented designs for clothing and jewelry. But toward the end of the book, author Harry Zuckerberg urges the reader to be concerned about and take concerted action toward the rebuilding of the Temple in Jerusalem.

Zuckerberg argues interestingly for the rebuilding:

WHY WE NEED THE THIRD TEMPLE

We look in our houses of worship and find our youth noticeably absent. They do not attend because they feel the services do not relate to their day to day problems.

The real problem we feel is that a state of mourning still exists for the destruction of the first and second Temples (Psalm 137). We find today instrumental music and dance on a very limited basis as a means of worship. The restriction of prayers primarily to reading and singing prayers is frustrating the personality of our people. It would appear that to reach fulfillment in prayer, we must find various ways to cater to the diverse talents and personalities amongst us. Those whose personality will not allow them to learn how to pray in the accepted form must find outlets for prayer. The third Temple would close this gap of emptiness that prevents millions of us from participating in prayer.

Most assuredly through the talents of each of us, additional methods of praising the LORD will be found, and the subject of prayer will take on new dimensions.

With the third Temple, we end our period of mourning, and a new world should begin for us. Our personality as a people will find new directions toward a brotherhood of man.[3]

It is certainly hard to quibble with renewing the vitality of Jewish prayer, giving a broader avenue for individual talents in the worship of God (Zuckerberg draws quite a bit from the Psalms about worship through music and dance), and bringing to an end Israel's lengthy mourning over the loss of the second Temple nineteen centuries ago. Finally, the new Temple of God, thinks the writer, would open up the possibility of a new "brotherhood of man."

Zuckerberg's views are unique, and his theology very original. He wants a brotherhood of man to be caused by God finding a suitable "resting place" on the earth (the Temple). He wants to involve the Jewish youth very deeply in the project, and he wants to undertake the difficult task of persuading the world of Islam that the rebuilding of the Jerusalem Temple is for the best:

THE TEMPLE MOUNT

How can we think of building the temple with the revered Mosques on the Temple Mount in Jerusalem.

Our people are not concerned with the rebuilding and what it has to offer them. Why start up? Why look for trouble? The answer is a new world order with the brotherhood of man will result.

First we must interest people in rebuilding the third Temple. We propose as follows:

Step by Step—A Plan of Action

The building of models of the second Temple in 52 sections. That these models be sold to houses of worship the world over. That each week a section be placed in a rebuilding by a teen ager. The week of the 9th day of Av (commemoration of the destruction of the first and second Temple), should complete the rebuilding. That on the 9th day of Av, with the use of an attachment, a teen ager should pull a string causing the model to collapse.

We hope each week as the Temple is rebuilt, our youth will have a feeling of pride and a cause with a future.

The next step is to persuade the World of Islam that only by the rebuilding of the Temple will G__D find a resting place (Isaiah 66:1). That if G__D finds a resting place, the Divine Grace will dwell in Jerusalem, and a new and better world will commence. The present structures on the Temple Mount have not brought forth the peace and brotherhood of man we seek. G__D therefore is restless and we are having dissension, turmoil and instability in the world. Only a Temple built in accordance with the spirit of the patriarchs and prophets, and in accordance with Biblical direction can the basis of a new world order arise.

We submit the following:

> And remembereth the name of his Lord
> And prayeth.
> But ye prefer this present life,
> Though the life to come is better and
> More enduring.
> This truly is in the books of old,
> The books of Abraham and Moses.
>
> THE MOST HIGH
> THE KORAN[4]

The Koran does quote freely from the Old Testament, sometimes honoring the Scriptures, but Zuckerberg has his work cut out for him in persuading the Muslims that a more suitable house of God should replace their holy shrines.

Zuckerberg's philosophy about "a new world order with the brotherhood of man," rings very familiar to those acquainted with prophecy. As we have stressed through this book, the Antichrist will preach just such a doctrine, though it would not be quite fair to accuse Zuckerberg of furthering this awesome cause. Still, these high-sounding aspirations of a new world order in connection with the third Temple make one ponder. We must bear in mind that the third Temple is, in effect, the Antichrist's Temple, or at least it provides the backdrop for his most ambitious heresy—declaring himself to be God.

Involving the Jewish youth serves the good purpose of re-educating the future Jewish adult population about the Temple issue in all its fullness, but this would not be enough, of course, to effect the rebuilding. The Muslims will still object, and so Zuckerberg takes on the Muslims, complete with quotation of their scripture. He may stand alone in the world in his novel idea of inviting the Muslims to assist in rebuilding the Jewish Temple.

The Koran notwithstanding, Zuckerberg is probably in for some disappointments along the lines of Muslim cooperation with Israel. This would seem to be a greater miracle than the descent of the Celestial Temple of Fire from heaven. But Zuckerberg would like to see the Temple rebuilt "in our days."

The Low-Profile Movement

Rabbi Jaffee disclosed to writer George Cornell, in the Associated Press article quoted earlier, that there is sincere, scholarly research going on in Israel about the rebuilding. The archaeology progresses steadily, and the learned men continue to search for acceptable ways to progress toward this goal.

Step by Step—A Plan of Action

The scholars have not published their findings, but a low-profile consideration of the whole Temple matter is ever underway in Jerusalem. The Old Testament assures the world that the tenacious Jews are not easily defeated in their spiritual quests. The history of our own century shows that in the providence of God, these singular chosen people can accomplish great wonders. We have not heard all that is going on toward the rebuilding of the third Temple, and those of us who follow prophecy carefully can sense, in some way, an impending fulfillment.

God seems to move slowly with respect to human aspirations. The Jews would rather have had the Messiah sooner than two thousand years after God's covenant with Abraham. Christians would have chosen a sooner return of the Lord than the entirety of this lengthy Church age. Abraham desired a son long before God's chosen moment, and David would have liked to worship in the magnificent Temple of God constructed by his son.

We have always had to wait for God's own times and seasons. We have only His Word to depend on, but as we have seen throughout this book, His Word is very dependable.

What has been accomplished toward the rebuilding of the Temple of God since the original publication of *Satan in the Sanctuary?* Actually, a world of exciting things has occurred, if we take the long view necessary to waiting out prophecy. This whole section "updating" the impending fulfillment of the third Temple prophecy would not have been possible, of course, were it not for the steady progress toward God's moment. We have seen, in the time since our original publication, Jews approaching the actual Temple mount in prayer, the beginning of the construction of the Jerusalem Great Synagogue, the founding of organizations to promote the rebuilding of the Temple, the study of scholars toward this difficult goal, and a renewed interest, throughout the Jewish and Christian world, in the Tribulation Temple. We have seen a great deal of new preaching in the churches about the Temple and renewed efforts toward the evangelization of Israel. We have seen a war, the Yom Kippur War, in which there was a momentary threat of intervention by the superpowers and a global-level contest over Israel's very right to exist. We have seen shifting power struggles in the Middle East, an oil embargo, and an infinite number of suggestive movements of men toward the end times.*

Considering all that we have seen in the past four years, our position as expressed in the preface to the original edition of *Satan in the Sanctuary* remains the same: it is the hope of the authors to reach all readers—believers in Christ and unbelievers alike—with the message that God's Word goes on, oblivious to doubt, and that we today are in a position to see it fulfilled.

---

*See *The Coming Russian Invasion of Israel,* by McCall and Levitt [Chicago: Moody, 1974] for an understanding of how these events of the seventies lead toward the Tribulation period and its Temple.

6

The Bible Tells Me So

FOUR JERUSALEM TEMPLES are mentioned in the Bible. Two (Solomon's and Herod's) have come and gone, but two more (the Tribulation Temple and the Millennial Temple) are prophesied to be built in the future. The final Temple (Millennial) will be erected by the Lord Jesus Christ Himself when He establishes the Messianic kingdom, and it is described in detail in Ezekiel 40-48. But the Tribulation Temple must come first, and the evidence for its construction and use is found in four passages in the Bible—passages found in Daniel, Matthew, 2 Thessalonians, and Revelation.

We know that the Tribulation Temple will be built just as surely as our ancestors knew that the Messiah was coming. Daniel, whose reliability in predicting the future can be arithmetically shown (see below), prophesied both of these events along with many other revelations concerning the future of the world (Dan 9).

The Lord vindicated Daniel's vision when He quoted the prophet (Mt 24) and added a message of His own.

Then the apostle Paul followed suit (2 Th 2), referring to the Tribulation Temple. Finally, the apostle John added

78 *Israel and Tomorrow's Temple*

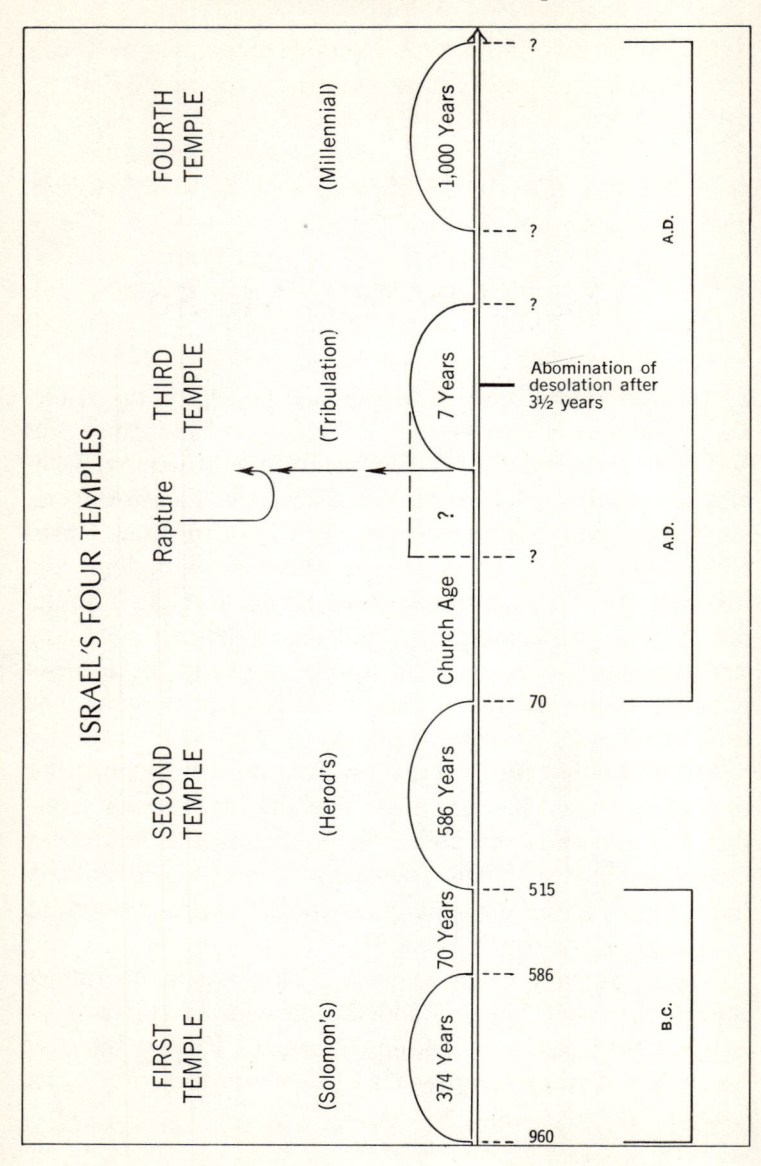

ISRAEL'S FOUR TEMPLES

FIRST TEMPLE (Solomon's)
- 374 Years — 960 B.C.
- 70 Years — 586

SECOND TEMPLE (Herod's)
- 586 Years — 515
- Church Age — 70 A.D.

Rapture

THIRD TEMPLE (Tribulation)
- ? — ?
- 7 Years — Abomination of desolation after 3½ years
- ?

FOURTH TEMPLE (Millennial)
- 1,000 Years
- ?

to the events surrounding the reestablishment of the Jerusalem Temple, and gave time figures corresponding to the ancient prophet's reckoning (Rev 11).

It should be said that Temple prophecy, as a field of prophecy, has been completely reliable. The first two Temples have come and gone on schedule, as it were—that is, in agreement with prophecies. It is hard for us, living in the modern world, to give the ancient prophets their due, considering their different circumstances and archaic language. But some of our ancestors were as lax as we are on this score. With all of the scriptural knowledge of the first century Jews, and their lip-service devotion to the Word of God, only a minority recognized their Messiah, the Second Temple destruction, and other forseen events.

Let's not be caught napping. Let's look into the Word:

> And after threescore and two weeks shall Messiah be cut off, but not for himself: and the people of the prince that shall come shall destroy the city and the sanctuary; and the end thereof shall be with a flood, and unto the end of the war desolations are determined. And he shall confirm the covenant with many for one week: and in the midst of the week *he shall cause the sacrifice and the oblation to cease,* and for the overspreading of abominations he shall make it desolate, even until the consumation, and that determined shall be poured upon the desolate (Dan 9:26-27, italics added).

A great deal is revealed in these two verses. Satan's evil prince—the Antichrist—will make a covenant with the people of Israel. The agreement is to last seven years (Daniel's "weeks" are actually seven-year periods). But the Antichrist will not keep his side of the covenant. In the midst of the seven years he will cause an end to the sacrifice and the oblation.

If the ancient practices of sacrifice and oblation are to be discontinued, then they must first be reinstituted. And this in turn requires a proper Temple.

John F. Walvoord says, "With the realignment of nations, Israel will enter into a covenant with the Gentile rulers of the Middle East, as anticipated in Daniel 9:26-27. . . . Orthodox Jews will apparently revive their ancient sacrifices and a temple will be provided."[1]

What is being described here are events in the coming tribulation period. Clearly, the Temple must be standing and in use by the middle of that period. As for the actual reconstruction time, it is not given. It could be built well before the middle of the tribulation period. We know only that it must be standing and operating for the Antichrist to carry out his actions against sacrifice and oblation, and those actions are prophesied to occur in the midst of the tribulation period.

No less an authority than our Lord corroborated Daniel's prophecy, and added still another piece of evidence for the establishment of a third Temple. In Matthew 24:15-16 Christ advised:

> When ye therefore shall see the abomination of desolation, spoken of by Daniel the prophet, *stand in the holy place,* (whoso readeth, let him understand:) then let them which be in Judaea flee into the mountains. (Italics added.)

The Lord said that the abomination of desolation referred to by Daniel would be in the holy place. The holy place was one of the two rooms in the original Temple design. These two rooms, designed and ordained by God, were the holy place (*ha-kodhesh*), and the most holy place (*kodhesh ha-kodhashim*). Exodus 26:33 makes the distinction between the two rooms, in the midst of a lengthy description of God's architectural instructions for the tabernacle.

The expression *holy place,* as used by the Lord, can only refer to this Temple room. The abomination of desolation will take place there, so the Temple must be standing. The Lord had already predicted the destruction of the second Temple, and here He predicts the establishment of the third. Surely the latter prophecy will prove as accurate as the former.

Also to be noticed here is the editorial commentary by the Holy Spirit that this passage is to be read with special understanding.

The apostle Paul also referred to the Tribulation Temple:

> Let no man deceive you by any means: for that day shall not come, except there come a falling away first, and that man of sin be revealed, the son of perdition; who opposeth and exalteth himself above all that is called God, or that is worshipped; so that he as God *sitteth in the temple of God,* shewing himself that he is God (2 Th 2:3-4, italics added).

The man of sin referred to here is elsewhere called the Antichrist or the wicked prince. He will be the chief opposer of God and all that belongs to God. He will seat himself in the Temple and proclaim himself God. He will demand the worship of all men. He will be "Satan in the sanctuary."

The Greek term in this Scripture for Temple is *naos,* which denotes the Temple building proper. The term *hieron,* used in other Scriptures, refers to the whole Temple site. Paul, then, very definitely locates the Antichrist as being in the sanctuary itself. This corroborates the Lord's reference to the holy place.

So, again, we must have the Temple to complete the picture of things to come. Nothing less than the rebuilding of the Temple sanctuary itself will satisfy these exacting prophecies.

John's fascinating Revelation also contains reference to the Tribulation Temple:

> And there was given to me a reed like unto a rod: and the angel stood, saying, Rise, and measure the temple of God, and the altar, and them that worship therein. But the court which is without the temple leave out, and measure it not; for it is given unto the Gentiles: and the holy city shall they tread under foot forty and two months (Rev 11:1-2).

So, in the midst of the section of Revelation that describes the tribulation period (chapters 4-19) a Temple appears. John is to measure it—not the general grounds which the Gentiles tread, but the Temple building proper; the *naos*. The altar and the worshipers are to be included in John's reckoning, but not the common courtyard, which will be desecrated by the Gentiles for forty-two months (three and one-half years).

How nicely this coincides with Daniel's calculations. Three and one-half years—indeed half of Daniel's final "week" (seven years)—will the holy city be despoiled after the abomination of desolation.

So here again we see that the Temple building must be standing at the halfway point of the tribulation.

Furthermore, in this passage we see that the Temple is sanctioned by God as an authentic Temple—an authorized place of worship. John is commanded to measure the "Temple of God." It is apparent that the tribulation Temple will stand and will be acceptable to God.

The Bible Tells Me So 83

In that God speaks of reckoning the building proper, the altar, and the worshipers, it is as if He welcomes the worship of the people in the Tribulation Temple, despite the ultimate actions of the Antichrist.

It is clear that this final reference combines well with the other three and pictures the same times. The time and place are well defined. The forty-two-month period foreseen by both Daniel and John is a persuasive example of biblical consistency.

DANIEL AND THE COMING PRINCE

Daniel's inspired foresight can be better evaluated if we double-check his accuracy. We have seen that God showed him the future situation concerning the Tribulation Temple and the Antichrist. But this is by no means the whole of the marvelous seventy-weeks-of-years prophecy.

The vision imparted to Daniel sweeps over history. It predicts the rebuilding of Jerusalem after the Babylonian captivity, the first coming and crucifixion of the Messiah, and the destruction of the second Temple, before dealing with the final tribulation period.

We might say that Daniel takes us from the end point of the prophecies of Jeremiah (600 B.C.) to the end of time.

This gives us a chance to check on Daniel. If he was right about the events that already have happened, there is good reason to suppose that he will be correct about future events.

We have looked at Daniel 9:26-27 for information about the coming tribulation period. Let's look back a verse for Daniel's version about Jesus, the Messiah. "Know therefore and understand that from the going forth of the commandment to restore and to build Jerusalem unto the Mes-

84   *Israel and Tomorrow's Temple*

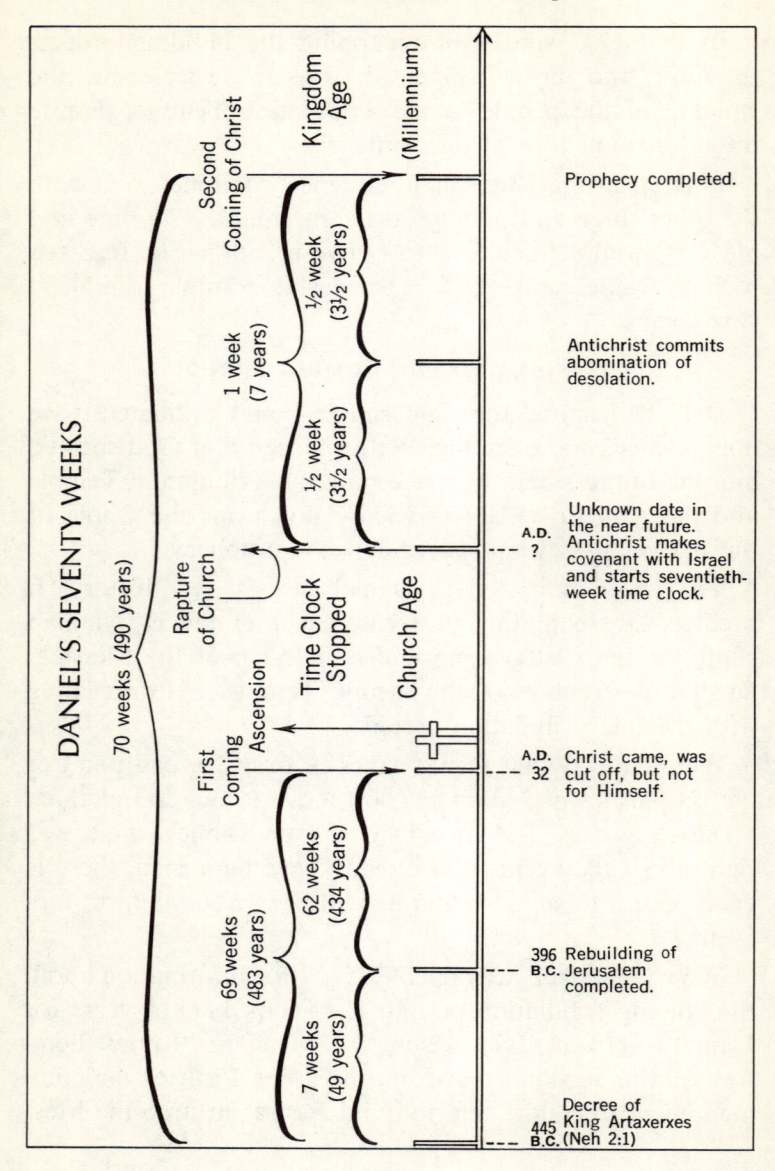

DANIEL'S SEVENTY WEEKS
70 weeks (490 years)

- **Second Coming of Christ** → Kingdom Age (Millennium) — Prophecy completed.
- ½ week (3½ years)
- 1 week (7 years)
- ½ week (3½ years) — Antichrist commits abomination of desolation.
- Rapture of Church — A.D. ? Unknown date in the near future. Antichrist makes covenant with Israel and starts seventieth-week time clock.
- Time Clock Stopped — Church Age
- First Coming / Ascension — A.D. 32 Christ came, was cut off, but not for Himself.
- 69 weeks (483 years)
  - 62 weeks (434 years) — 396 B.C. Rebuilding of Jerusalem completed.
  - 7 weeks (49 years) — 445 B.C. Decree of King Artaxerxes (Neh 2:1)

The Bible Tells Me So 85

siah the Prince shall be seven weeks, and threescore and two weeks" (9:25).

Or to paraphrase, "The Messiah will come sixty-nine weeks after the commandment to rebuild Jerusalem."

Imagine making such a statement six centuries before Christ!

The very idea of predicting some kind of commandment that Jerusalem should be rebuilt must have left students of Daniel incredulous. The Jews were the captives of Babylon at the time and could not reasonably look forward to restoring their vanquished capital.

Yet, some two centuries later, such a commandment was issued, in the form of a royal decree by King Artaxerxes, who gave permission to the governor Nehemiah to restore the Jewish capital. (Neh 2:1-6).

We know the date of that benevolent proclamation; Nehemiah 2:1 sets it "In the month Nisan, in the twentieth year of Artaxerxes," which makes it 445 B.C.

Before going on, we should realize that Daniel's "weeks" are actually seven-year periods. The Hebrew term used denotes "sets of seven," and we know that years are meant since the restoration of Jerusalem took exactly forty-nine years (finished in 396 B.C.) and this corresponds with the prophet's "seven weeks." Also, it would have been impossible to prophecy that a great city would be rebuilt in just seven weeks' time.

And we should know that Daniel regarded a year as having 360 days, which was Jewish tradition for calculations. We can see this in Revelation 11:3 where the three and one-half year tribulation is given as 1,260 days (three and one-half years times 360 days per year.)

We can see at a glance that Daniel's calculations are accurate. His "sixty-nine weeks," meaning sixty-nine sets of seven years comes out to 483 years (360-day years). Since the decree to rebuild Jerusalem came in 445 B.C., the projection certainly puts us right in Jesus' generation.

But Daniel was more precise than that, at least according to the classic *The Coming Prince,* written by Sir Robert Anderson a century ago.

Anderson showed in his remarkable work that Daniel was accurate to the *exact day!* While Anderson's proof does rest on a number of reasonable assumptions, it is difficult to refute. It has mostly been attacked on the grounds that it is "too perfect." In any case, it is a fascinating exercise to review and serves to demonstrate that we might do well to take Daniel seriously.

Here are the results derived from Anderson's calculations:[2]

1. Daniel prophesied that the Messiah would come 173,880 days after Artaxerxes' decree:
   69 "weeks" = 483 years (69 x 7)
   483 years x 360 days (Jewish year in prophecy) = 173,880 days.
2. The actual day of the decree was March 14, 445 B.C. We know from Neh. 2:1-6 that the decree was issued "in the month of Nisan, in the 20th year" of Artaxerxes' reign (465-425 B.C.) We can assume that the decree was dated on the first of Nisan because "The first of Nisan is a new year for the computation of the reign of kings and for festivals." (MISHNA, treatise "Rosh Hashanah.") The first of Nisan, 445 B.C. fell on March 14 (Royal Observatory, Greenwich, Eng.)
3. The actual day of the coming of the Messiah was April 6, A.D. 32.
   The "coming of the Messiah" was the day on which

Jesus made His triumphal entry into Jerusalem and was proclaimed King by the Jews. This is given in Zech. 9:9.

John the Baptist and Jesus began their ministries during the 15th year of the reign of Tiberius Caesar (Luke 3:1, 3, 21) whom we know began his reign in A.D. 14. Thus, our Lord started His ministry A.D. 29 and continued, as we know, for 3 years before His triumphal entry: thus A.D. 32 was the year.

We have it from John 12:1 that the Lord went to Bethany, on the outskirts of Jerusalem, "six days before the Passover," and from John 12:12 that the triumphal entry was the "next day."

Passover is always celebrated on 14 Nisan, which was Thursday, April 10, in A.D. 32 (Royal Observatory). So the Lord came to Bethany April 4 (6 days before Passover) which was a Friday. The meal with Lazarus at Bethany must have been a Sabbath dinner. The "next day" could not have been Saturday (the Sabbath still in effect, Jesus and the Jews would have rested) so the Lord made His triumphal entry on Sunday, April 6, A.D. 32.

To recap all that, Anderson says (1) that Daniel foresaw that there would be 173,880 days between the issuing of Artaxerxes' decree and the coming of the Messiah; (2) that the decree was issued March 14, 445 B.C.; (3) that the Messiah came officially on April 6, A.D. 32.

If Daniel is correct to the exact day, there should have been 173,880 days between those two dates. Anderson works it out this way: From March 14, 445 B.C. to April 6, A.D. 32 is 477 years and 24 days. But we must deduct one year because 1 B.C. to A.D. 1 is only one year. So we have 476 years and 24 days. 476 years x 365 days (in our Julian calendar) = 173,740 days. Adding in the extra 24 days = 173,764 days.

That doesn't quite do it. But peculiarities of our calendar, the Julian calendar, must also be considered. We have leap year every four years; therefore, there were 119 leap years during the period (476 years divided by 4 equals 119). So, adding in the extra 119 days,

$$\begin{array}{r} 173{,}764 \\ +119 \\ \hline 173{,}883 \text{ days} \end{array}$$

That's too many days. But Anderson went so far as to calculate the slight inaccuracy of our Julian year as compared with the true solar year. The figures, from the Royal Observatory, show that our year is about 1/128 of a day longer than the true solar year. We therefore skip leap year every 128 years on our calendar. Three such leap years must be skipped during Daniel's prophetic period of 483 years. Thus we subtract 3 days:

$$\begin{array}{r} 173{,}883 \\ -3 \\ \hline 173{,}880 \end{array}$$

And we see that Daniel was accurate to the exact day.

Our purpose here is not to check Anderson's arithmetic, but to underline the very real accuracy of the prophet Daniel. We have based our prediction of the future construction of the Tribulation Temple and the events surrounding it largely on this seventy-weeks prophecy. If

Daniel's other predictions were mistaken, we would have a weak argument.

But it appears he was exactly right on the coming of the Messiah. It is hard to doubt him on the Tribulation Temple.

We are now in the position of having been warned by a prophet. We're not the first ones. God's voice was heard through the prophets again and again, and particularly in connection with the Temples of Jerusalem. But, surprisingly, through this long history of the Temple site, the prophets were largely scoffed at. People must have read these Scriptures, but they somehow thought they would muddle through, and the prophecies wouldn't come to pass.

Are we doing the same thing?

Let's look back at the whole story of the Jerusalem Temple site.

7

Moses to Moshe—A Bloody Site

THIRTY-FIVE HUNDRED YEARS of blood, sweat, and tears have gone into the Temple site.

Compare this figure for a moment with other time stretches in history. The United States has been a country for two hundred years. Great Britain, which at one time administrated the empire upon which the sun never set, counts about nine centuries.

The grand traditions of Greece and Rome—those great civilizations we commonly regard as ancient—lack a thousand years against the age of the Temple site events.

It is hard to appreciate in these times, but from Moses' liberation of the Jews from Egypt in 1500 B.C., to General Moshe Dayan's recovery of the temple site in A.D. 1967, the Jews have never forgotten that singular ideal—the great Jerusalem Temple.

They have twice before achieved their ideal, and twice lost it. Both of the earlier temples were prophesied in the Bible, as was the destruction of both. The same Bible also prophesies the construction and destruction of the Tribulation Temple. Finally, prophecy establishes the millennial Temple, Christ's ruling house on the earth.

Moses to Moshe—A Bloody Site

Let's look a moment at the heartbreaking history of the Temples.

THE FIRST TEMPLE

"Upon one of the mountains which I will tell thee of" (Gen 22:2).

The Bible begins its chronicle of the history of mankind "In the beginning"—a long time ago. But one doesn't have to turn a great many pages before coming to God's first direction as to the Temple site.

In the book of Genesis God directs Abraham to sacrifice his only son, Isaac, on a certain mountain. This turns out to be Mount Moriah, the very site of the later Temples. The Dome of the Rock is now standing on the spot where Abraham willingly prepared to sacrifice Isaac.

That fine story is typical of the pathos and heartbreak that were to follow on this piece of ground. One has to appreciate that Abraham waited a lifetime for the birth of his son. He waited on the Lord even past his wife's normal time of childbirth, until she was far too old to bear a child. He had a son by his wife's maid, but this was not acceptable to God, who assured Abraham that his prayer for a son by his own wife would be answered.

And when it miraculously was, Abraham was asked to kill the child.

There came a happy ending, of course. God was testing Abraham; Isaac was spared. Because Abraham's faith was so complete, God made his loyal servant a wonderful promise which we can easily see fulfilled today: "By myself have I sworn . . . because thou . . . has not withheld thy son . . . I will multiply thy seed as the stars of the heaven . . . *and thy seed shall possess the gate of his enemies*" (Gen 22:16-17, italics added).

Possessing the gate and erecting a temple are quite different matters, however, as we shall see.

Some four centuries after Abraham, Moses was preparing the wandering Jewish nation to conquer the promised land. They had enjoyed divine deliverance from slavery in Egypt, but had wandered forty years in the desert enroute to Israel. They had worshiped and sacrificed, not always to God's liking, as they traveled.

But now God gave to Moses specific directions concerning the first temple: "There shall be a place which the LORD your God shall choose to cause His name to dwell there" (Deu 12:11).

God's mind was made up. There was to be a ban on sacrificial worship at any other location once the Jews held the chosen site: "Take heed to thyself that thou offer not thy burnt-offerings in every place that thou seest: but in the place which the LORD shall choose" (Deu 12:13-14).

Like their father, Abraham, they waited. The Jews took the promised land, but there followed the enormous task of creating a nation before a Temple could be built. Centuries passed while the former slave-nomads cultivated the arts of trade and commerce, agriculture, and self-government. Borders were defended, wars were fought, and the Jews praised their God, ever mindful that somewhere in their hard-won land was the site of their future Temple.

The rule of judges gave way to the rule of kings. The young nation was blessed with a succession of capable monarchs, the second of whom—the great King David—captured the city of Jerusalem, then held by the Jebusites.

Now the Temple stage was set. David, a national hero as a boy when he slew Goliath, a marvelously talented poet and musician, the composer of the Psalms, a dancer of exotic dances to God, and an able king of the Jews for almost forty years, made Jerusalem his capital. We are still seeing the results of this choice. His first concern in Jerusalem, as he told the prophet Nathan, was, "See now, I dwell in a house of cedar, but the ark of God dwelleth within curtains" (2 Sa 7:2). The Jews had continued their worship in a temporary tabernacle, or tent, lacking a proper Temple.

Nathan, speaking with the knowledge of a prophet of God, encouraged David to go ahead with the Temple plans. "The LORD is with thee," he advised (2 Sa 7:3).

The reaction of God to David's enthusiasm for the sacred project was to promise, as He did with Abraham, that David's posterity would endure; more, that the very kingdom of Christ would be founded upon David.

Jesus, David's descendant ("of the seed of David according to the flesh" Ro 1:3) was indeed "crowned" at Jerusalem, but with a crown of thorns. The Davidic covenant, as this promise is called, is immutable, however, and as we have seen from prophecy, Jesus is to reign, truly the king on earth.

But David was not to oversee the actual construction of the temple. He disqualified himself as the years went on, by being too much of a soldier. On one occasion he committed a sin of pride by conducting a military census of the nation. He wanted to know the exact number of Hebrew men who "drew the sword."

David's servant Joab could see the folly here; God would be provoked by the king's conceit. "Why then doth my lord require this thing?" he questions David. "Why will he be a cause of trespass to Israel?" (1 Ch 21:3).

But David had his way. Israel's standing army was counted and proved to boast of 1.5 million soldiers.

Joab was right about God's attitude toward this indiscretion. A pestilence of terrible proportions hit the little kingdom, and seventy thousand men died of the disease. An angel of the Lord, reports 2 Samuel 24, was carrying out this penalty, but was told by God to desist as the epidemic reached Jerusalem.

By this difficult means God revealed the actual temple site; the angel was stopped right at the threshing floor of Araunah, a Jebusite national who respected the king. The prophet Gad advised David to buy the site from Araunah and erect an altar there to God. This would stop the plague.

Araunah told David to take what he wished and sacrifice it; there was no need for payment. Araunah was honored by the presence of the king; "Let my lord the king take and offer up what seemeth good unto him . . . the LORD thy God accept thee" (2 Sam 24:22-23).

But David insisted on giving a price for the grounds; "Nay; but I will surely buy it of thee at a price: neither will I offer burnt-offerings unto the LORD my God of that which doth cost me nothing" (2 Sam 24:24). And he paid for the land.

There, on Mount Moriah, where Abraham had offered Isaac, King David built an altar to God. This was the mountain of Genesis 22:2 "which I will tell thee of."

And that became the temple site.

David, now old and tired, began to gather the special materials and finances to build the great Temple on this site. In a conversation of touching candor he assigned his son Solomon the actual task, explaining his own role and failure:

> Then he called Solomon his son, and charged him to build a house for the LORD God of Israel. And David said to Solomon, My son, as for me, it was in my mind to build a house unto the name of the LORD my God; but

the word of the LORD came to me saying, Thou hast shed blood abundantly, and hast made great wars: thou shalt not build a house unto my name, because thou hast shed much blood upon the earth in my sight. Behold, a son shall be born to thee, who shall be a man of rest; and I will give him rest from all his enemies round about: for his name shall be Solomon [from *shalom,* "peace"], and I will give peace and quietness unto Israel in his days. He shall build a house for my name; and he shall be my son, and I will establish the throne of his kingdom over Israel for ever. Now, my son, the LORD be with thee; and prosper thou, and build the house of the LORD thy God, as he hath said of thee. Only the LORD give thee wisdom and understanding, and give thee charge concerning Israel . . . . be strong and of good courage; dread not, nor be dismayed. Now, behold, in my trouble I have prepared for the house of the LORD an hundred thousand talents of gold, and a thousand thousand talents of silver [a talent has been estimated as high as $10,000]; and of brass and iron without weight; for it is in abundance: timber also and stone have I prepared; and thou mayest add thereto. Moreover there are workmen with thee in abundance, hewers and workers of stone and timber, and all manner of cunning [skillful] men for every manner of work. Of the gold, the silver, and the brass, and the iron, there is no number. Arise therefore, and be doing, and the LORD be with thee (1 Ch 22:6-16).

David also approached the princes of the land—the commerce leaders and the powerful among the people—and commanded them to help Solomon in his great work:

> Is not the LORD your God with you? And hath he not given you rest on every side? For he hath given the inhabitants of the land into mine hand; and the land is subdued before the LORD, and before His people. Now set

your heart and your soul to seek the LORD your God; arise therefore, and build ye the sanctuary of the LORD God, to bring the ark of the covenant of the Lord, and the holy vessels of God, into the house that is to be built to the name of the LORD. (1 Ch 22:18-19).

"SOLOMON IN ALL HIS GLORY"

The new king was the equal of his father. God had promised him wisdom, and he surely was one of the most intelligent and accomplished men ever to grace a throne. A statesman of great skill, an enlightened philosopher, the author of Song of Solomon, Proverbs, and Ecclesiastes, and the husband of some seven hundred wives (plus three hundred concubines) Solomon is unsurpassed even in fiction as a colorful and masterful leader.

He established a new level of law and order in his country, and God maintained the peace as Solomon multiplied the wealth and importance of little Israel among the powerful nations of the day. He cultivated alliances with Egypt, Phoenicia and the great cities of the Near East: Tyre, Sidon, Babylon, and Nineveh. He established a mighty mercantile fleet on the Red Sea and sent mining expeditions into Arabia for precious metals.

And he adorned Jerusalem with the Temple of God.

The great Temple was not merely a single structure, but a quadrangle with a number of buildings. The main sanctuary, which housed the holy place and the most holy place, was ninety feet long, thirty-five feet wide, and four stories high. It was made of cedar beams overlaid with pure gold inside and out. Gold was spread lavishly about; on the beams of the main ceiling, on the posts, the doors, and the walls, on the candelabra, the lamps, the snuffers, the spoons, and the various artifacts. Precious stones were in-

Moses to Moshe—A Bloody Site

laid everywhere. Two gold-plated cherubim guarded the ark of the covenant.

The labor involved was tremendous. We must appreciate that the porch before the main structure rose 180 feet—which would qualify this structure as a modern skyscraper. Huge blocks of solid stone had to be raised to this breathtaking twenty-story height. The construction took a force of 150,000 laborers seven years to accomplish.

The dedication ceremony must have been something to behold! King Solomon had a brass scaffold built in the midst of the court, from which he prayed a dedicatory prayer before the people.

This prayer, recorded in 2 Chronicles 6, reaches magnificent heights of gratitude and entreaty to God, and is in character not unlike the Lord's Prayer. Solomon, too, asks forgiveness for his people's trespasses and deliverance from evil. He recounts for the benefit of the mesmerized congregation the promises of God to his father David and the passing down of the Temple responsibility to himself.

He speaks to God in front of the assembly:

> And he stood before the altar of the LORD in the presence of all the congregation of Israel, and spread forth his hands . . . and said, O LORD God of Israel, there is no God like thee in the heaven, nor in the earth; which keepest covenant, and shewest mercy unto thy servants, that walk before thee with all their hearts (2 Ch 6:12-14).

He prays with great humility: "But will God in very deed dwell with men on the earth? Behold, heaven and the heaven of heavens cannot contain thee; how much less this house which I have built!" (v.18).

He dedicates the Temple: "Now, therefore, arise, O

LORD God, into thy resting place, thou, and the ark of thy strength" (v.41).

God appeared to Solomon by night, shortly after his prayer, and accepted the holy Temple: "I have heard thy prayer, and have chosen this place to myself for a house of sacrifice" (2 Ch 7:12).

A miracle accompanied the opening of the Temple for normal worship. "The house was filled with a cloud . . . so that the priests could not stand to minister . . . the glory of the LORD had filled the house of God" (2 Ch 5:13-14). This harked back to Moses' interviews with God as recounted in Exodus 19:9, "And the LORD said unto Moses, Lo, I come unto thee in a thick cloud" and in 20:21, "And the people stood afar off, and Moses drew near unto the thick darkness where God was."

So the Temple was established, and it became a wonder of the ancient world. Centuries passed and the house of God prevailed.

And that might have made an end to the story of unremitting tragedy that is the history of the Jews, but the people fell from God's favor. As the years went on, the Jews forgot the terrible struggle of their ancestors for the promised land and for the Temple.

Their ever-present prophets were on the job; Isaiah and particularly Jeremiah, constantly reminded the people that God required complete faith and strict adherence to their heritage. They foresaw terrible destruction in Israel because of the superficial worship. They warned of God's wrath.

Four hundred years after King Solomon dedicated the great Jerusalem Temple it was sacked and burned to the ground by an invading army. The Babylonians conquered Israel, broke down the walls of Jerusalem, set a torch to

Moses to Moshe—A Bloody Site

the city, and slaughtered young and old, men and women alike, right in the Temple sanctuary.

> They mocked the messengers of God, and despised his words, and misused his prophets, until the wrath of the LORD arose against his people, till there was no remedy. Therefore he brought upon them the king of the Chaldees, who slew their young men with the sword in the house of their sanctuary, and had no compassion upon young man or maiden, old man, or him that stooped for age: he gave them all into his hand. And all the vessels of the house of God, great and small, and the treasures of the house of the LORD, and the treasures of the king, and of his princes; all these he brought to Babylon. And they burnt the house of God (2 Ch 36:16-19).

This enthusiastic conqueror was not actually the king of the invaders, but merely a field marshal; the "captain of the guard," according to 2 Kings 25:8, which also relates this sad incident. The king of Babylon at the time was Nebuchadnezzar, who had personally supervised the siege of Jerusalem.

The city and the Temple were taken by stages during Nebuchadnezzar's rule. Babylon was extremely strong in those times. According to 2 Ki 24:7 "The king of Babylon had taken [conquered] from the river of Egypt unto the river Euphrates all that pertained to the king of Egypt." Little Israel was in a squeeze as usual, between the colossi, Egypt and Babylon.

The eighteen-year-old King Jehoiachin of Israel inherited this unhappy situation. He was in office only briefly when Nebuchadnezzar and the hosts of Babylon laid siege to his capital. The adolescent king went out into the field to surrender, bringing his mother and officers of the court with him.

On this occasion Nebuchadnezzar did not have Jerusalem burned, but thought that a mass deportation of the Jews would take care of the Jewish nation once and for all.

The book of Kings tells the cruel story of the ravaging of a once great nation:

> And he [Nebuchadnezzar] carried out thence all the treasures of the house of the LORD . . . and cut in pieces all the vessels of gold which Solomon king of Israel had made in the temple of the LORD, as the LORD had said. And he carried away [back to Babylon in chains] all Jerusalem, and all the princes, and all the mighty men of valour, even ten thousand captives, and all the craftsmen and smiths: none remained, save the poorest sort of people of the land (2 Ki 24:13-14).

What a terrible vengeance! The Babylonian king took the lifeblood of Israel as slaves. He purposely chose, not just soldiers and government leaders, but the talented workmen of the little country. Israel could not possibly bounce back. He left them only their poor and indigent.

The passage also relates that Nebuchadnezzar took the young king and his family as slaves. He then placed Jehoiachin's uncle, Zedekiah, on the throne in Jerusalem.

With all of this the indomitable Jews were not subdued. Eleven years passed as Israel reorganized, and then the puppet king rebelled against Babylon.

It was hopeless.

This time Nebuchadnezzar knew no leniency. He surrounded Jerusalem in a heartless siege that cut off the food supply of the populous capital. The Jewish army deserted, slipping out of the city by night. The king tried the same thing but was apprehended by a detachment of the army of the Chaldees. They brought him to his former mentor.

Moses to Moshe—A Bloody Site

Zedekiah's fate was to see his sons killed before his eyes and then to be blinded and dragged to Babylon in brass fetters.

It was then that the thorough captain of Nebuchadnezzar's guard came on the scene, obviously with orders to utterly obliterate Jerusalem.

Field executions of the highest ranking government and military officials were rampant. And the cruelest blow of all, the destruction of the Temple, was completed to the extent that the thirty-four-acre stone quadrangle vanished without a trace. Virtually nothing was left standing.

According to the Bible the Jews deserved God's judgment. With each successive king there reappears the ominous Scripture, "And he did that which was evil in the sight of the Lord" (2 Ch 36:5, 9, 12).

The destiny of the Jews has always been special. They "have and have not" in great measure according to their behavior toward the Lord. Their very survival through the ages attests to God's special dealings with them. Where are those other great nations today? Where are the mighty hosts of Babylon, or the blood-thirsty Chaldees? The Philistines, the Hittites, the Moabites, and a hundred worthy powers have vanished, while the Jews—persecuted and dispersed without end—have survived to retake their capital and their holy Temple site.

The Jews who lost their mighty first Temple could not have said they weren't warned. Isaiah agonized over the future 150 years before the Babylonian siege: "Thy holy cities are a wilderness, Zion is a wilderness, Jerusalem a desolation. Our holy and our beautiful house, where our fathers praised thee, is burned up with fire: and all our pleasant things are laid waste" (Is 64:10-11).

But Isaiah was regarded as an ill-tempered old man.

Later, in the first year of the reign of the terrible Nebuchadnezzar of Babylon, the prophet Jeremiah focused attention on the future events like tomorrow's newspaper:

> Thus saith the LORD of hosts; because ye have not heard my words, behold, I will send and take all the families of the north [the Chaldees, etc.] . . . and Nebuchadnezzar the king of Babylon, my servant, and will bring them against this land, and against the inhabitants thereof . . . and will utterly destroy them, and make them an astonishment, and an hissing, and perpetual desolations. Moreover I will take from them the voice of gladness, the voice of the bridegroom, and the voice of mirth, and the voice of the bride, the sound of the millstones, and the light of the candle. And this whole land shall be a desolation and an astonishment (Jer 25:8-11).

You would think that when the prophet gives names and places, and when his analysis agrees reasonably with foreseeable political situations, he would be taken very seriously. But what happened to Jeremiah is truly remarkable and perhaps instructive.

He was jailed.

To speak against the Temple and Jerusalem was tantamount to treason, and Jeremiah, the voice of the Lord, was made a political prisoner.

His trial was a curious affair. The priests, like the Pharisees who tried our Lord, insisted on the death penalty. Had not this miserable prophet compared the great city of Jerusalem to Shiloh in his rantings? (Shiloh, the site of the tabernacle of God before Solomon's time, had been ravaged by military invasion.)

The elders present were more circumspect. When had anybody gotten away with killing a prophet of God? Wouldn't it be better to avoid blood on their hands? Remember Micah, and Urijah—prophets of the ancient days—who prophesied against Jerusalem accurately enough.

And so they imprisoned their prophet.

The Jews were lulled into a false sense of security by their several successful defenses of the capital over the four centuries since Solomon. The Egyptians, the Syrians, and the brutal Assyrians had all assaulted walled Jerusalem, with its strategic highlands. They had all failed to take the city.

But, Jeremiah had pointed out, the defenders had the power of God with them in those reverent days. Things were different now. The Jews had turned from God over the centuries. Did they think that the Almighty could not turn the tide against them? Did they suppose that they would be forever guaranteed impregnability because of the devoutness of their ancestors?

Jeremiah lived to be a heartbroken witness to the exact fulfillments of his prophecies.

We find in Josephus, a Romanized Jewish historian of the first century A.D., an interesting reference to a miracle on the scene of the destruction of Solomon's Temple. It's as if God did indeed take a hand. Josephus wrote in connection with the destruction of the second Temple, which we shall look at presently, but he did take notice of a certain special event that had to do with the first temple: "As for Titus [the Roman general who destroyed the second temple in A.D. 70], those springs that were formerly almost dried up when they were under your power—since he is come—run more plentifully than they did before."[1] Josephus is talking about the springs of water outside Jerusalem. The water supply was always critical for the invading army in that hot region. The historian noted that Titus and his Roman troops had plenty of water available from springs which had formerly been so miserly that the water had been rationed:

> You know that Siloam, as well as all other springs that were without the city, did so far fail, that water was sold by distinct measures; whereas they now have such a great quantity of water for your enemies, as is sufficient not only for drink both for themselves and their cattle, but for watering their gardens also.[2]

The occupying Romans had water galore, for their civilian pursuits and, most importantly, for the troops who besieged Jerusalem. And now the historian harks back to the time of Nebuchadnezzar's attack: "The same wonderful [remarkable] sign you had also experienced formerly, when the fore-mentioned king of Babylon [Nebuchadnezzar] made war against us, and when he took the city and burnt the Temple."[3]

This information certainly underlines Jeremiah's warning that God can control military matters, and will use the Gentiles ("Nebuchadnezzar the king of Babylon, my servant" Jer 27:6) to punish His people and will even comfort them while they are at it.

Josephus is not a Bible writer, of course, but is a well-documented secular historian to whom we owe credence for many corroborated reports of the times.

Jeremiah took little satisfaction in seeing the accuracy of his prophecy. He became the saddest of men over the destruction of the holy city, the starvation of the people, and the deepest cut of all—the burning of the house of God.

In a fervor of misery he wrote the book of Lamentations, setting to the music of a dirge the desolation of Jerusalem. This majestic moment, one of the peaks of the great literature of the Old Testament, cannot be sufficiently quoted here for the reader to appreciate its true magnitude. "The Lord was as an enemy," cries Jeremiah:

> He hath swallowed up Israel, he hath swallowed up all her palaces: he hath destroyed his strong holds, and hath increased in the daughter of Judah mourning and lamentation. And he hath violently taken away his tabernacle, as if it were of a garden: he hath destroyed his places of the assembly. . . . The Lord hath cast off his altar, he hath abhorred his sanctuary, he hath given up into the hand of the enemy the walls of her palaces. . . . The Lord hath purposed to destroy the wall of the daughter of Zion. . . . . Her gates are sunk into the ground; he hath destroyed and broken her bars: her king and her princes are among the Gentiles: the law is no more; her prophets also find no vision from the LORD (Lam 2:5-9).

Too late now for the visions of prophets! Jeremiah's reportage is touching:

> The elders of the daughter of Zion sit upon the ground, and keep silence. . . . They have girded themselves with sackcloth: the virgins of Jerusalem hang down their heads to the ground. Mine eyes do fail with tears. (Lam 2:10-11)

So the brilliance of Jeremiah is finally consummated in a woeful funeral dirge. His assignment was limited to foreseeing the tragedies surrounding the first Temple. Imagine his tears if he could have foreseen the events of the second Temple—the literal starvation of a million people and still another desolation of the holy site.

But even the lamentations following that catastrophe would be mild. Suppose Jeremiah could look ahead, as we are now able to do, to the destruction of the third Temple—the Tribulation Temple. Now there's something to lament! The entire earth consumed in Armageddon. Perhaps a billion casualties this time.

Can we learn from these debacles? Not at all, according to the prophets. We still are scoffing. We treat Daniel, Paul, John, and Jesus Christ no better than those patriarchs of ancient Israel treated Isaiah and Jeremiah.

There is little difference in our time. The Jews in Jeremiah's day might have avoided their punishment by turning back to God. The setup is the same this time. Christ will claim God's own before the tribulation period, the Scriptures say, and they will be spared the terrible events to come.

It's even easier this time. Since the first coming of Christ it is necessary only for us to ask. We no not have to fulfill a complex law. We do not have to pay for past deeds.

Jeremiah put it very well at the conclusion of his Lamentations: "Thou, O LORD, remainest for ever; thy throne from generation to generation. . . . Turn thou us unto thee, O LORD, and we shall be turned" (Lam 5:19-21).

The Jews remained in Babylonian captivity for some seventy years, as Jeremiah had also prophesied. Then, as God made it possible for them, they started to put the pieces of Israel back together once again. The dream of every Jew was to rebuild the house of God on its appointed site.

Let's look now at the drama of the second Temple.

8

I Will Fill This House with Glory

SO NOW THE MAIN BODY of the Jewish nation was exiled in Babylon. The date of Nebuchadnezzar's first siege was 605 B.C. The Jews were carried off in groups until 586 B.C.

The underrated book of Jeremiah remained in the ruins of Jerusalem, considered not worthy of deportation by Nebuchadnezzar's armies. But his visions were to carry on. Among the captives interned in Babylon was a youth of the royal court named Daniel.

Daniel was a devout worshiper of God, longing for freedom and remaining in constant prayer for Israel throughout his long life. He was to see the entire seventy years of captivity pass and to witness the return to Jerusalem and the founding of the second Temple. Too bad, in all his patience and faith, that he could not have read the clear statements of Jeremiah 29:10-14:

> Thus saith the LORD, That after seventy years be accomplished at Babylon I will visit you, and perform my good word toward you, in causing you to return to this place [the holy land] . . . And I will turn away your captivity, and I will gather you from all the nations, and from all the places whither I have driven you, saith the LORD;

and I will bring you again into the place whence I caused you to be carried away captive.

Apparently Jeremiah's unpopular views had been suppressed in the interests of national security; and Daniel, denied the Word of God, prayed for freedom for seventy years.

The honored prophet did live to read the revelations of Jeremiah near the end of the captivity period. He was finally able to state, "I Daniel understood by books the number of the years, whereof the word of the LORD came to Jeremiah the prophet, that he would accomplish seventy years in the desolations of Jerusalem" (Dan 9:2). Daniel's wait for freedom and his trust in God rival the steadfast faith of Abraham.

Daniel's prayer concerning the return and the rebuilding is a masterful passage in his wonderful book:

> And I set my face unto the Lord God, to seek by prayer and supplications, with fasting, and sackcloth, and ashes: and I prayed unto the LORD my God, and made my confession, and said, O Lord, the great and dreadful God, keeping the covenant and mercy to them that love him, and to them that keep his commandments; we have sinned, and have committed iniquity, and have done wickedly, and have rebelled, even by departing from thy precepts and from thy judgments. . . . O Lord, righteousness belongeth unto thee, but unto us confusion of faces, as at this day; to the men of Judah, and to the inhabitants of Jerusalem, and unto all Israel, that are near, and that are far off, through all the countries whither thou hast driven them, because of their trespass that they have trespassed against thee. O Lord, to us belongeth confusion of face, to our kings, to our princes, and to our fathers, because we have sinned against thee (Dan 9:3-8).

I Will Fill This House with Glory

He entreats for Jerusalem and the Temple:

> O Lord, according to all thy righteousness, I beseech thee, let thine anger and thy fury be turned way from thy city Jerusalem, thy holy mountain: because for our sins, and for the iniquities of our fathers, Jerusalem and thy people are become a reproach to all that are about us. Now therefore, O our God, hear the prayer of thy servant, and his supplications, and cause thy face to shine upon thy sanctuary that is desolate, for the Lord's sake (vv. 16-17).

Daniel concludes with a supplication. "O Lord, hear; O Lord, forgive; O Lord, hearken and do; defer not, for thine own sake, O my God: for thy city and thy people are called by thy name" (v.19).

In answer to this magnificent prayer, God gave Daniel the seventy-weeks-of-years prophecy. Daniel reports that the angel Gabriel came to him as he was finishing his prayers: "And he informed me, and talked with me, and said, O Daniel, I am now come forth to give thee skill and understanding" (v.22).

And that he did. As we have seen, the seventy-weeks prophecy with its scope of millennia is unassailable.

In view of his humble appreciation of Jeremiah, Daniel must have been staggered by his own vision of world history complete through Christ to the millennium.

Soon after the prophecy everything changed. In a war between Persia and Babylon, the Babylonians succumbed, and to King Cyrus of the victors went all the property of Babylon. This included the cream of the Jewish nation and the prophet Daniel.

This was good for the exiled Jews. Cyrus was sympathetic—a model conqueror who always respected the religious persuasions of his adversaries. He allowed the Jews free emigration to their holy city and had no objections to their rebuilding the Temple. Gabriella Rosenthal recounts in her book *Jerusalem*:

> Forty years later, [after the war] the Persian King Cyrus who had conquered Babylon, allowed the Jews to return. Only the bravest, the idealists—and certainly not the richest, although these generously supported the project—dared to embark on this undertaking. To rebuild a ruined city and resettle a wasteland is an arduous task. It was made even harder by the Samaritan inhabitants, and time and again hampered by political intrigue. When the main altar had been rebuilt, the construction of a new temple commenced.[1]

It appears that it was no easier to rebuild the temple in that century than it is now. The foreign feet that always tread God's city invariably are an obstacle. The Jews held a brick in one hand and a sword in the other.

The reconstruction, according to Ezra, was under the direction of Zerubbabel, heir to the Jewish throne, and Joshua, the high priest. The former was a descendant of the house of David and is mentioned in the genealogy of Jesus (Mt 1:12).

The two had their work cut out for them. These were not the happy times of Solomon. Jerusalem was as desolate as the earlier prophets had warned, and the returned populace, reared in Babylon, was not very pioneer-minded. The two leaders did, however, succeed in rebuilding a smaller Temple, but the people had mixed reactions.

Ezra reports:

> And all the people shouted with a great shout, when they praised the LORD, because the foundation of the house of

the LORD was laid. But many of the priests and Levites and chief of the fathers, who were ancient men, that had seen the first house, when the foundation of this house was laid before their eyes, wept with a loud voice. . . the people could not discern the noise of the shout of joy from the noise of the weeping of the people (Ezra 3:11-13).

The sages of the first Temple, who must have been in their nineties, could not abide the more modest version.

The Almighty corroborates their opinion through the prophet Haggai, reporting on the scene: "Who is left among you that saw this house in her first glory? And how do ye see it now? Is it not in your eyes in comparison of it as nothing?" (Hag 2:3).

But good things can come in smaller packages. Haggai continues: I will shake all nations, and the desire of all nations shall come: and I will fill this house with glory, saith the LORD of hosts. . . . The glory of this latter house shall be greater than of the former, saith the LORD of hosts: and in this place will I give peace (2:7-9).

Relative peace did prevail then, for centuries, and little is heard of the second Temple until the period of the Maccabees (165 B.C.). Apparently the Jews maintained their precarious national heritage though their land remained a playing field for the great military contests of the civilized world. Alexander the Great and armies of every nationality passed through at will, robbing and raping, but the Jews continued their Temple worship and sacrifices all the same.

As to the Temple itself, it is not celebrated in secular chronicling, as are the more grand temples of Greece and Rome. The Greco-Syrian ruler Antiochus Epiphanes, a merciless warrior, desecrated the house of the Lord in

167 B.C. by sacrificing a sow on the altar. The Maccabees, freedom fighters of the period, rededicated the Temple, creating the Feast of Chanukah in the process. This feast of dedication was faithfully celebrated by Jesus (Jn 10:22) and is still commemorated by today's Jews.

But the next major happening in the history of the Temple site belongs to Herod the Great, the neurotic Roman-appointed king of the Jews, in the century preceding Christ.

Herod's private life was a horror story of paranoid executions of his own wives and children, and endless suspicions of just about everybody in Jerusalem. Publicly, he liked to be celebrated as some kind of wise and just king of Solomonic bearing.

He certainly fell far short of the illustrious King Solomon but did have traits in common with the great sovereign. Herod, too, preferred a beautiful capital and a luxurious court, and maintained a building program which virtually broke the national economy. In the manner of Solomon also, he fell into foreign ways, preferring the refined culture of the Greek to the earthy and practical manner of the Jew.

Herod decided that the Hellenic ways offered a better unity for his kingdom than the troublesome Jewish traditions. He raised mighty Greek buildings in Jerusalem— a theatre and an amphitheatre—and decorated God's city with monuments to Augustus and other pagans. He sponsored Greek-style musical contests and sporting events. He tried to interest the Jews in Roman gladitorial combats.

The chosen people were scandalized by nude statues and the naked wrestlers in Herod's games. The king was plainly a vassal of Rome, and his subjects plotted revolution against that power day and night. Jerusalem was likely the superlative tourist attraction of its time, with its unusual mixture of architecture, politics, manners, and morals.

Then Herod proposed to replace the house of God. Zerubbabel's Temple was too small, he said. Jerusalem, with its new (Greek) grandeur, should have a fitting monument to the God who had inspired such fascinating lore as the learned Jews could tell. Herod utilized the Jewish "legends" as an excuse to spend the public funds on his masterpiece, gaining the approval of the Jewish leaders and many of the people.

The project was passed off as a "remodeling" of the original second temple, but was in reality a complete rebuilding. The main structures were in place in eight years time, but the adornments took another seventy years.

There is no doubt that this shrine rose to world importance for its beauty, but it asked the Jews to swallow some obvious paganism. Massive Corinthian columns rose to support the main structure, and the detested eagle of Rome dominated the entrance, defying the Jewish prohibition on graven images.

Herod continued to Hellenize the other cities of Palestine with expensive public buildings unimpressive to the Jews. Revolutionists plotted against him constantly and the aging king took to brutal public punishments of the suspects. He disguised himself on occasion, went out among the people and did his own police work. He managed to die a natural death, just at the time Christ was born, but his project of embellishing the Temple went on for the better part of a century.

During the ministry of Jesus and well beyond, Hellenic "improvements" were constantly added until the Jerusalem Temple was truly a marvel, even among the magnificent architecture of its age.

The Temple's value as a military fortress was not unnoticed. Huge walls surrounded the site and the city—a comforting addition to an area that had seen battles and lootings from time immemorial. A tall tower rose in the foreground of the site. Josephus noted: "The temple was a fortress that guarded the city, as was the tower of Antonia a guard to the temple; and in that tower were the guards of those three."[2]

With all of the Greek tradition of gorgeous architecture, and the Roman tradition of plenty of soldiers on the scene, the Temple was still exemplary in its primary purpose—the worship of God. The Day of Atonement—the once-a-year owning up of the Jewish people to God for their sins—was observed faithfully and with great fervor. Steckoll writes:

> It is said that there is no person holier than the High Priest. There is no place holier than the Holy of Holies [area] of the Temple. There is no holier time than during the Day of Atonement. And nothing holier than the Ineffable Name of the Almighty God, the name which it is forbidden to utter. These four come together and it was the custom, before the destruction of the Temple, for the High Priest to utter the Name of God on the Day of Atonement in the Holy of Holies. Such was the awe in which the annual occasion was held that the belief grew, belief which in turn became dogma, that, should the High Priest have the slightest impure thought while pronouncing the Name of God in the Holy of Holies, the immediate destruction of the world would ensue.[3]

It was perhaps this kind of premonition of doom, which could hardly be respected by serious scholars of God's

I Will Fill This House with Glory

Word, that caused the Jews to overlook again the warnings of their prophets concerning the Temple. The 500-year-old structure, made even more formidable by Herod's builders (remade, if the truth be told) was considered invincible.

But it was only as invincible as its illustrious forerunner.

Haggai's promise that the second Temple would be more greatly glorified by God than the first (Hag 2:6-9), was more than justified. Herod's work improved it, of course, but the prophecy's fulfillment lies in the fact that Jesus Christ, the Jewish Messiah, graced this Temple with His presence and His great teachings. This was the very site of those stirring gospel scenes; here Jesus chastised the money changers and animal sellers; here He taught the Word of God to a hostile and skeptical melee; here He was accused and tormented by those "who knew Him not."

Jesus did not comment on the Temple itself, except to prophecy its destruction. The Pharisees were horrified at Jesus' prediction that "There shall not be left here one stone upon another" (Mt 24:2), but the Lord was as much a prophet as a fulfillment of prophecy.

Daniel, too, foresaw the Lord's appearance in the second Temple in the great seventy-weeks prophecy (Dan 9:25-26).

Zechariah, Haggai's contemporary at the time of the reconstruction after Babylon, adds a fascinating note to the second Temple destruction. In Zechariah 11:7-14, he discusses the Lord's good Shepherd (Jesus; see Jn 10:11). In the prophet's vision the good Shepherd is given the wages of thirty pieces of silver. This terrible undervaluation is the same figure Judas accepted to betray Christ (Mt 27:3-10). God considers the payment so repugnant that He has it thrown away, to the potter in the Temple. Then

He breaks the two shepherd's staves with which He has kept the surrounding nations from overrunning Israel and by which He has kept them united. The image is of wolves and sheep.

The vision illustrates the wrath of God caused by the Hebrew rejection of their Messiah.

The Jewish nation had a history of turning from God, and will have it in the future. With the first Temple they rejected God and His blessings as the years went on, and they lost their Temple and were deported to Babylon for seventy years. With the second Temple, as we shall see, they lost the sanctuary again and were dispersed throughout the world for nineteen centuries, not to have a Jewish Israel until A.D. 1948.

With the third Temple—the coming Tribulation Temple—they will make a covenant in good faith with the Antichrist. But he will break the covenant, and desecrate the Temple. This time will be the last time. Then Armageddon will fall.

For the benefit of those unfamiliar with, or unrespectful of prophecy, Jesus, standing directly in the Temple, spelled out the coming destruction still again. He specified that the reason was again rejecting of the gifts of God; particularly rejection of the Messiah:

> O Jerusalem, Jerusalem, thou that killest the prophets, and stonest them which are sent unto thee, how often would I have gathered thy children together, even as a hen gathereth her chickens under her wings, and ye would not! Behold, *your house is left unto you desolate.* For I say unto you, Ye shall not see me henceforth, till ye shall say, Blessed is he that cometh in the name of the Lord. And Jesus went out, and departed from the temple. (Mt 23:37-24:1, italics added).

Destruction of the Second Temple

They should have listened to Jesus. The catastrophe of the destruction of the second Temple is almost beyond imagination.

At least 1.1 million Jews died in the five-month siege of Jerusalem by the Roman legions.

Approximately 600,000 starved to death in the streets. Their bodies were thrown over the city walls at the rate of 4,000 per day.

Josephus records cannibalism among the panicky and starving 3 million people crammed within the city walls.[4]

And the Temple was razed so thoroughly that our Lord's prophecy was completely fulfilled—not one stone was left upon another.

Nobody really wanted that to happen. Titus, the Roman general who conducted the siege, was not a barbarian; he did want to spare the magnificent Temple. The people he annihilated with typical Roman efficiency, but the Temple was the crown jewel of the Middle East, and he gave orders to spare it.

But in the heat of the ferocious hand-to-hand fighting between the maddened defenders and the Roman regulars, a torch was thrown, reports Josephus.

The Jews were having enough trouble among themselves without the siege. Although the Jews held a promising military position—Jerusalem had a succession of three mighty walls, not to mention the strategically high-grounded Temple site—they could not organize a common defense. Warring factions destroyed the vast stocks of food stored in the city against just such a siege. Josephus laments, "Almost all the corn (maize or wheat) was burnt, which would have been sufficient for a siege of many years."[5]

Titus had purposely sealed off the city at Passover, which accounted for the swollen population. Pilgrims who had come great distances to celebrate the feast were trapped in that ghastly scene of streets clogged with corpses, the wounded starving among the dead, and the increasing lack of space to suffer in as the defenders retreated.

Finally the Jews had to fall back to the Temple site and the adjacent Hill of Zion. There, walled in, perhaps a million people, sick and dying, awaited the Roman legions.

There was simply inadequate ground for each person to stand on, if they could stand. The Temple buildings must have been packed full. They must have had to pile themselves up. There was no hope of food, no hope of removing the dead, no room for the defenders to fight.

The Jews trusted the Temple to divine intervention. When asked to surrender, they refused, saying:

> That yet this Temple would be preserved by Him that inhabited therein, whom they still had for their assistant in this war, and did therefore laugh at all his [Titus'] threatenings, which would come to nothing; because the conclusion of the whole depended upon God only.[6]

Titus was not much concerned about the Almighty but did, according to Josephus, want to preserve the magnificent Temple.

The Romans continued to advance and, inevitably, were able to enter the Temple grounds. We can imagine that scene of carnage as the exhausted defenders took on the invaders in hand-to-hand combat. Casualties must have run very high on both sides, and the combatants must have been knee deep in corpses, freshly dead and otherwise.

I Will Fill This House with Glory

This was not the pitched battle of modern warfare with an aim-and-fire style; the soldiers, with no room to hide, must have literally hacked each other into submission with swords and knives. We can imagine the horror confronting the civilian population of Jerusalem, infirm as it now was, caught helpless on the battlefield.

The Jews had no place to fall back to anymore. They feared destruction of the Temple if they surrendered. They were surely in no shape to fight, but they had to stand their ground.

We don't know the casualty figures of the battle for the Temple site, but we can calculate the military losses for the five months of the siege by subtracting the losses from starvation from the total casualty figures as given by Josephus.

In combat one-half million Jews were killed.

We can put this in modern terms by comparing it to the Vietnam conflict. In eight years, over the whole of Vietnam, America lost 55,000 men, from all causes. In fact, to have a casualty figure even comparable to that of the Jews in this incredible holocaust, we would have to total up all of America's losses in all of her wars from the Revolutionary War of 1776 to the present.

In five months in Jerusalem the Jews lost more than a million.

The Second Temple Burns

Josephus reports that Titus gave implicit orders that the Temple not be touched in the final battle. He may have pictured that the defenders, under horrible losses, might give up the fight. He must have wanted to see an early end to the Temple site attack because the Roman casualties must also have been high.

And it might well have been a feather in his political cap to subdue the Jews while keeping that lovely "ornament" intact; how satisfying it would have been to report back to Rome, "Jews defeated—Roman headquarters now billeted in Temple sanctuary." The former commander of Titus' troops became emperor, after all, and Titus was his heir.

But the Temple burned. The devastation was complete. Josephus puts the blame on an anonymous Roman soldier:

> These Romans put the Jews to flight [where?] and proceeded as far as the holy house itself. At which time one of the soldiers, without staying for any orders, and without any concern or dread upon him at so great an undertaking, and being hurried on by a certain divine fury, snatched somewhat out of the materials that were on fire, and being lifted up by another soldier, he set fire to a golden window, through which there was a passage to the rooms that were round about the holy house . . . on the north side of it.[7]

We can wonder about the accuracy of Josephus' war correspondence, but he could have seen it all with Titus from the vantage point of the Antonia Fortress, which overlooked the Temple site. He was normally to be found behind the lines of the winning side, rather than in the heat of the battle.

Nevertheless the Temple was gone, not to be replaced by the Jews to date. From that moment the Jews became what they were until 1948—an entire race of people with no home address. They still have no central shrine. We can appreciate their current wish to rebuild the Jerusalem Temple.

Josephus thought that the destruction of the Temple

I Will Fill This House with Glory

was in reality a retributive act of God, and he discovered a remarkable fact that is borne out under modern investigation: The first and second Temples were destroyed on the same day of the year.

He reasons:

> It was fate that decreed it [the destruction] so to be, which is inevitable, both as to living creatures and as to works and places also. However, one cannot but wonder at the accuracy of this period thereto relating; for the same month and day were observed, . . . wherein the holy house was burnt formerly by the Babylonians.[8]
>
> I suppose that had the Romans made any longer delay in coming against these villains the city would either have been swallowed up by the ground opening upon them, or been overflowed by water, or else been destroyed by such thunder as the country of Sodom perished by, for it had brought forth a generation of men much more atheistical than were those that suffered such punishments; for by their madness it was that all the people came to be destroyed.[9]

The date of the destruction of both Temples, 656 years apart, was the ninth day of Av, in the Jewish calendar, corresponding to mid-August. The devout Jews continue to recognize this date of sorrow.

Should we watch for the Tribulation Temple to fall on that same date in some future year?

Josephus saw himself as some kind of latter-day Jeremiah, having warned the Jews to capitulate earlier in order to save the Temple. He had, in fact, gone to John, (according to his own report) the rebel commander, and had given him a practical example from the Bible—Jeconiah's surrender to the Babylonians:

> But still, John, it is never dishonorable to repent, and

amend what hath been done amiss, even at the last extremity. Thou has an instance (example) before thee in Jeconiah, the king of the Jews, if thou hast a mind to save the city, who, when the king of Babylon made war against him, did, of his own accord, go out of this city before it was taken, and did undergo a voluntary capitivity with his family, that the sanctuary might not be delivered up to the enemy, and that he might not see the house of God set on fire;[10]

And after all, John might become some sort of national hero:

On which account he is celebrated among all the Jews, in their sacred memorials, and his memory is become immortal, and will be conveyed fresh down to our posterity through all ages.

This, John, is an excellent example in such a time of danger.[11]

This Romanesque expediency apparently did not impress the Jewish general. We might say, considering Josephus' friendly relations with the enemy, that the passage smacks of war propaganda. Perhaps the Romans were counting on the influence of Josephus to calm the rebellion and save the Temple, but the negotiator seems only to have saved himself.

More Temples

Now the Romans thought the Jews were utterly subdued, and for the most part they were. Josephus sailed back to Rome with Titus after the devastation of Jerusalem and marched in a triumphal procession that exhibited Jewish captives and artifacts. He ended up with an apartment in the royal palace, supplied by his old friend Ves-

I Will Fill This House with Glory

pasian, the emperor, and lucrative property back in the holy land. He then (about A.D. 75) set down the public relations material we have been quoting, calling the work *The Wars of the Jews.*

Back in Jerusalem there was desolation, but faithful Jews still resided there and in the surrounding countryside. There were basic changes in Judaism then that prevail to our present time and will prevail until the Tribulation Temple is in use. The rabbi replaced the priest, the local synagogue replaced the Temple; and particularly, sacrifice was discontinued because of the lack of a fitting setting.

For two generations peace prevailed.

Then came Hadrian, one of the most brilliant of the Roman emperors. Like King David, he was a most accomplished artist, a good singer and dancer, and a player of the harp. He wrote well, prose and poetry, and is generally conceded to have been a competent, tactful administrator of the enormous Roman Empire.

But he had quirks.

Hadrian was a passionate Panhellenist who resented the Jews and their detested offspring, Christianity.

He calculated that the infestation of monotheism emanated from Jerusalem, and he determined, like so many before him, to obliterate the name of that city from human memory.

His was not the method of military might. He was more thorough.

He changed the name of the holy city to Aeolia Capitolina and set out to make it a showplace of Roman culture and religion.

And he sent his builders to construct the Temple of Jupiter on God's holy mountain.

The Jewish Temple site was to be used for pagan worship. Hadrian had chosen it purposely. Soon, he thought, there would be no further trace of Judaism. The upstart Christianity would be without even the ruins of its holy place.

The Greco-Roman culture that he personally worshiped would prevail throughout the known world.

What could be done? Could the Jews allow such outrages?

Doggedly, hopelessly, the Jews armed again for war with Rome.

A leader arose—Simeon Bar Kochba—who claimed to be the Jewish Messiah and therefore invincible. It was to be the last effort of the Jews to recover their homeland by force until 1948.

This time there was no central shrine to defend, so the Jews spread out the rebellion through Israel. They held on for three years while the legions resolutely dug them out over the whole of the country.

This began the great dispersion of the Jews throughout the world which did not come to an end until 1948. It is remarkable that the time-honored Jewish rituals survived this dispersion, in earthly terms, but it was largely the work of faithful law codifiers and teachers of the troubled time. The greatest of these, Rabbi Akiba ben Joseph, is a prime example of the tenacity and courage of the Jew.

He survived the siege of Jerusalem in A.D. 70 and continued to teach the oral law. He could recite the Pentateuch by heart, and his fame spread through Israel. In A.D. 95 he was chosen, with Gamaliel and others, to go on a diplomatic mission to Rome. The Jewish delegation was successful in talks with Emperor Nerva, and a heavy tax was repealed.

I Will Fill This House with Glory

Akiba's painstaking organization and exposition of Jewish theology and law, still considered valuable, continued completely through the rebellion against Hadrian, and even after the emperor's proclamations against the teaching of the Jewish law. Akiba proclaimed Bar Kochba as the Messiah and was allied with him in the revolt.

Several rabbis who continued to teach in spite of the prohibition were executed, but the honored Akiba, now ninety-five years old, was jailed.

In jail he continued to teach. His fellow prisoners, and visitors, if they were allowed, must have heard rare wisdom from the aged scholar, whose life span reached almost back to Christ.

After three years of this he was tried and convicted. The ninety-eight-year-old patriarch was executed for teaching the Jewish law.

The Romans destroyed 985 towns in Palestine and slew 580,000 men, according to the Roman chronicler, Dio Cassius. Starvation again began to take its toll as agriculture ceased in the face of the advancing legions. The "Messiah" was killed defending Bethar.

When the Jews gave up the fight, so many were sold as slaves that their price fell to that of a horse. Civilians lived the lives of fugitives, hiding in caves and underground channels. The Romans did a complete mop-up throughout the little country. Every citizen was regarded as a combatant.

Archaeologists have recently uncovered evidences in caves by the Dead Sea that some sought refuge even in that inhospitable place.

Now Hadrian pounced on the vanquished enemy with another of those solutions to the "Jewish problem." A learned student of history, he well knew the recuperative powers of the Jews, and he set out to annihilate their religious heritage.

He forbad circumcision, the observance of the Sabbath and the holy days, and the public performance of any Jewish ritual. A new and heavier tax was levied on the Jews. They were allowed in Jerusalem, or rather Aeolia Capitolina, on only one fixed day each year, when they might weep at the Temple site (the "Wailing Wall").

On the bloody ground of Jerusalem, Aeolia Capitolina rose, disgusting the Jews with its shrines to Jupiter and Venus, theatres, baths, and the inevitable garrisons of the Roman legions. The Temple of Jupiter stood squarely on the hallowed site.

The Temple of Jupiter was well built, and it lasted a long time. In fact, it outlasted the Roman Empire.

At some point in the decline of Rome and the advance of Christianity it was remodeled and used as a Christian church. While the history of this period is sketchy, we do know that the Temple site apparently boasted of a Christian church when the Christian patriarch Sophomius welcomed the Caliph Omar into Jerusalem in 638. Justinian added a church, now the Aksa Mosque, in the sixth century.

It is likely that Hadrian's pillars supported the roof at that time, because those pillars are still standing today, supporting the Dome of the Rock, according to some scholars.[12] After 1,800 years they are doing just fine.

The probability is that the basic structure by the Romans was remodeled as the church and then again as the dome.

The Moslem Arabs took Jerusalem sometime in the seventh century. The Dome of the Rock dates from A.D. 691.

I Will Fill This House with Glory

The Moslems have never had troubles comparable to the Jews at the Temple site, but it was not entirely peaceful either.

The Crusades, those worldwide holy wars, brought the professing Christians of Europe against the populous Syrian and Egyptian Moslems in many a bloody battle on the temple site during the twelfth through fourteenth centuries. The dome bore a golden cross for nearly a century, creating a Christian symbol on a Moslem dome superimposed on a Roman temple built on a Jewish site.

And that was not nearly the end of it.

The Crusaders thought the Dome was Solomon's Temple originally and named it Templum Domini. Continuing a Roman tradition, they garrisoned the tough Knights Templar in the Aksa Mosque to guarantee the passage of devout European Christians who made pilgrimages to the holy site.

We can imagine the devotion of those hearty believers who journeyed from far-off Scandinavia, England, France, and Spain in those medieval days, to pray in what they thought of as the very building graced by Jesus Christ.

But the knights eventually lost the Temple grounds to the Moslems, who certainly had a shorter supply line, and from that time—the fourteenth century—the Temple site had remained in non-Jewish, non-Christian hands until 1967.

The Turks, in their various wars with the Arabs, sometimes captured the ground, but always had to relinquish it. The Dome survived and, with various improvements and remodelings, is essentially the same today.

At the time of the First World War, Palestine became a British mandate, and Prime Minister Balfour, in response to the Zionist movement, declared that the Jews should be permitted to return to Palestine as their homeland.

They did this, in considerable numbers. And there were still Jews present in Israel whose ancestors either had never left their promised land, or had been able to return sometime in the passage of the centuries.

The rest is within memory.

Twenty-five years ago, the time of the Gentiles began to come to a close, as the Jews prevailed in their war for independence. At that time Jerusalem once again became an armed camp; it was bayonets instead of swords, and jeeps instead of horses, but the old city must almost have shuddered under the all too familiar agonies of combat.

And in 1967 the Jews recovered the Temple site.

Now, after seeing this story—after following the history of this piece of ground from the time of Abraham's offered sacrifice—we can see the meaning of this repossession.

The Jews remember, as they study their rich heritage, the terrible forty-years journey to the promised land from Egypt; the great days of David and Solomon when the mighty first Temple graced Jerusalem; the horrors of the Babylonian assault and captivity; the painful rebuilding under Zerubbabel, and Nehemiah, when the builders carried swords to the site to hold off the Samaritans while they worked.

And they can well remember the decimation of Israel under the crushing rule of Rome; the starvation of an entire people; the destruction of the second Temple; the humiliation of Hadrian's pagan house on their sacred site, and the terrible, endless dispersion of Jewry throughout the world.

They want to rebuild their Temple. That's understandable.

We Christians can remember the same chapters of history. The significance of the Jews rebuilding their Temple

I Will Fill This House with Glory

has even greater import to those who await the King of kings as a sign of His return.

We remember what God said through Daniel, Paul, John, and our Lord Jesus Christ. We will not fail to heed the great Jewish prophets who foresaw the cataclysmic events connected with the third Jerusalem Temple.

If we can write the history of the great Temples of Jerusalem from God's Word, we can utilize the same source to write the future. As the Lord pointed out, "The scriptures must be fulfilled" (Mk 14:49).

We rejoice in the coming of the Tribulation Temple, for the sake of its part in the second coming. But, too, we realize that all of the bloodshed and all of the tears of thousands of years must culminate in still more war on this site.

For the Christian there is no fear because the rapture will precede the coming holocaust. For others, the Armageddon will make this chronicle of Temple bloodshed pale.

We certainly can see the future from God's word.

Read on.

9

The Antichrist—
"War I Give unto You"

HE MAY BE ALIVE TODAY.

We have seen that the third Jerusalem Temple, the Tribulation Temple, will be on stage for the final act of God's drama about the earth. Now let's look at the villain of the piece. He does his fatal work in the Temple, and he brings the world total destruction.

He is a political leader of great acumen—virtually a sorcerer. He is engaging and appealing. He captures the loyalty of what is left of the world after the rapture, and he becomes a kind of inverse messiah. The world trusts him with its problems, and he certainly succeeds in putting it out of its misery.

He is an egomaniac to make Hitler, Napoleon, and all the Caesars fade into soft-spoken modesty. He steadily gathers power and influence through his public relations man, the False Prophet, and he finally proclaims himself—not king nor president nor world ruler—but God Almighty.

The Antichrist—"War I Give unto You" 131

He does demonstrate seemingly supernatural powers, but they are not from above. The best that can be said of him is "the devil made him do it."

Our Lord lamented in John 5:43 that the world would receive this "messiah" who would come, not in the name of God, but in his own name.

That name is "Antichrist," signifying his contrast with our Lord.

This chapter is mainly for unbelievers, who will have to deal with the Antichrist and his system of world domination. The believers will be gone via the rapture (see next chapter) before his appearance.

Perhaps God's people will watch the world events as the Antichrist dominates, but they will be watching from heaven, not earth. The best seat for this particular play is in the balcony.

If you are an unbeliever and you do not come to the Lord before the rapture, you might as well know whom to watch for. There are many world leaders these days, each with his own brand of egomania, but the Antichrist has certain definite characteristics.

The key is his "seven-year plan" for the Middle East. Daniel tells us, "He shall confirm the covenant with many for one week [of years]" (9:27). Another main characteristic is that the Antichrist is European—from out of a revived Roman Empire. Daniel 7:23-24 specifies the "fourth kingdom," which is Rome, the fourth world-dominating power in biblical history.

For other details, let's consult the biblical seers.

We find out, from the intriguing description of the Antichrist in Revelation 13:1-8, that he is a ten-headed beast and that he recovers from an apparently fatal wound.

The ten heads represent the last conglomeration of political power, anchored in Europe and the Mediterranean area, and led by the Antichrist. Daniel also saw this tenfold combination of power (7:24). (It is fascinating to compare the visions of Daniel and John, so many centuries apart, yet with so much in common.)

So we have a ten-nation confederacy in Europe and the Mediterranean area at the time of the Antichrist.

Hal Lindsey says flatly, "We believe that the Common Market and the trend toward unification of Europe may well be the beginning of the ten-nation confederacy predicted by Daniel and the Book of Revelation."[1]

Since the publication of Lindsey's book, meetings have been held about the extension of the Common Market to include ten nations. The setting: Rome.

The apparently fatal wound, spoken of in Revelation 13:13, is a masterwork of good publicity for the Antichrist. It appears, from Revelation 13:14, that the Antichrist himself suffers a mortal wound, and then is miraculously resurrected. It is not a case of a serious wound healing up, but more of a "coming back to life" as described in the Scripture.

This counterfeits the resurrection of our Lord and establishes the Antichrist's power overnight.

We can imagine the possibility of an assassination attempt on the Antichrist, political assassinations having the vogue they do these days. The tremendous display of emotion and grief that will be exhibited when the Antichrist is cut down will only be exceeded by the astonishment when he comes right back up.

For impact, Lindsey considers what the world reaction would be if President John F. Kennedy were to reappear suddenly on the political scene, "recovered" from his tragic assassination.

The Antichrist—"War I Give unto You" 133

Obviously the Antichrist will gain world recognition by this event.

Supernatural power? Possibly. John notes that the Antichrist "doeth great wonders" (Rev 13:13), and "he maketh fire come down from heaven on the earth in the sight of men" (13:13). "All the world wondered after the beast" (13:3). "Who is like the beast? Who is able to make war with him?" (13:4).

Satan is identified loud and clear as the source of the Antichrist's magic in Revelation 13:4: "And they worshipped the dragon which gave power unto the beast."

Recognizing the Antichrist before he steps forward with his "Seven-Year Plan" is not easy. Whereas Jesus' birthplace was clearly given—Bethlehem was named in the Scriptures—the Antichrist's origin is unclear. It is certain that his political dominance is with Rome (or Europe as a new Roman Empire). Daniel 9:27 identifies him as the future prince of the people who would destroy the second Temple, and we know that Rome did this (A.D. 70).

There is a less clear intimation that the Antichrist will originate out of the Middle East; Daniel stops in the midst of his prophetic vision of the ultimate end of the Hellenizing powers (Greco-Syrian) to describe a "king of fierce countenance" who sounds like a first-class Antichrist (Dan 8:23-24).

We might say that the Antichrist will have some Middle Eastern background and will rise in power on the European political scene.

He might even be alive today.

Why not? The Middle East is certainly ready for solutions to its problems. The European confederacy isn't hard to spot. The Tribulation Temple, which the Antichrist will desecrate, is in the offing.

Admittedly these situations might hang on, or even repeat together at some future time. Possibly the Tribulation Temple will be built at once, but then stand there by the century awaiting its desecrator.

But the presence of other prophesied phenomena of the end times—earthquakes, the Russian-Egyptian alliance, world ecumenism—combined with the "ideal" Antichrist setup, makes even conservative Bible scholars think twice.

It is beyond the scope of this book to list the issues that qualify our generation to be the last. Suffice it to say that there's never been a better time to think it over.

THE BAD NEWS

This is the doctrine of the Antichrist, who will borrow the principles of religion to bolster his world dictatorship.

This is his "gospel."

First of all, God and Christ have got to go, in his view. John saw this and set it down clearly: "And every spirit that does not confess Jesus is not from God; and this is the spirit of the antichrist" (1 Jn 4:3 NASB).

Instead, he establishes a personality cult, based on worship of himself. He definitely demands the worship of the entire human race. Only those few who receive Christ during the tribulation period are not tempted (and they have their troubles.) His religious cult is by far the most successful, in terms of membership, in history: "All [unbelievers] who dwell on the earth will worship him" (Rev 13:8 NASB).

He will even have his own version of John the Baptist. Called the "false prophet" in Revelation 16:13, this promotion-minded front man will apparently utilize the power of Satan to gather the worshipers, and will be capable of quite a few fascinating illusions. Bringing down the fire

The Antichrist—"War I Give unto You" 135

from heaven and so forth will be routine. His masterpiece will be the creation of a lifelike replica of the Antichrist, capable of speech—perhaps a robot with computer capabilities.

The Antichrist is certainly one of a kind, but the two archvillains of the Bible predict him to some degree. Judas Iscariot, who sold Christ to the world for thirty pieces of silver, and Antiochus Epiphanes, who desecrated the second Temple by sacrificing a sow on the altar, both illustrate traits of the Antichrist.

"The son of perdition" is a description used by both Jesus and Paul to describe different people. The Lord is referring to Judas (Jn 17:12) while Paul is prophesying the activity of the Antichrist (2 Th 2:3-4).

Antiochus exalted himself in the Jerusalem Temple and caused the normal worship to cease, just as the Antichrist will.

But our man in Satan is the true master. Let's look at the Antichrist's actions as they will be.

I Am God

Modesty is not his long suit. He is fanatically sold on himself and his abilities.

He is a man of tremendous energy and action; a diplomat and a peacemaker, a messiah and a field marshal.

He will institute a new version of the Pax Romana—the Roman Peace—which will be no improvement over the old one. By amassing military power and politically expedient relationships throughout the world, he will guarantee the peace—at a price. His solution for the Middle East situation will work brilliantly, for a time—three and one-half years, to be precise. The astute Daniel observes that the Antichrist "by peace shall destroy many" (Dan 8:25).

He will establish a world economy wherein every person will have to participate. Revelation 13:16-18 reveals that every citizen will bear a mark on either his right hand or his forehead; it will be the number 666. Without this mysterious mark no individual will be permitted to buy or sell anything.

This was written in a time when people certainly could not imagine the possibilities of numbers, like Social Security or credit card numbers, having economic significance.

All this mess will bring on Armageddon.

Now back to the Tribulation Temple, built and being used for worship on its designated site in Jerusalem. It will become a prime target for the Antichrist.

What better setting for the headquarters of his own religion?

The Jews will have put up with the Antichrist until he gets around to the Temple. They will have been thankful for his handling of their political situation, and they will render him such allegiance as doesn't interfere with their normal worship of God.

But they'll draw the line when he enters the Temple.

The Antichrist will do this in a reckless way. He will already have virtual control of the world. Like many a tyrant before him, he will begin to resent the independence and private worship of the Jews. Something about Jewish worship has always disturbed dictators.

He will have a throne placed in the sanctuary of the Jerusalem Temple, and he will sit on it and declare himself to be God Almighty!

That's it for the Jews.

And the Temple. And everything else.

The Jews will not tolerate this desecration. They will arm and fight.

The Antichrist—"War I Give unto You" 137

And the Antichrist will regard this as his chance to finish them off. Another tyrant with another solution to the Jewish problem!

The Antichrist will gather a tremendous army, such as the world has never imagined. Revelation 16:13-14,16 chronicles the mobilization of a virtual world army. The Antichrist may possibly realize that he is embarking on a traditionally hazardous project in making holy war on the Jews. In any case, he assembles the vast might of "the kings . . . of the world," and he gathers them together in that quiet, level plain called Armageddon.

Among the personalities attending that great battle is Jesus Christ.

But not the meek and mild Jesus as he is so often characterized. This time the Lord comes for battle:

> And I saw Heaven opened, and behold a white horse; and He that sat upon him was called Faithful and True, and in righteousness he doth judge and make war. His eyes were as a flame of fire, and on his head were many crowns; and he had a name written, that no man knew, but he himself. And he was clothed with a vesture dipped in blood: and his name is called The Word of God. And the armies which were in heaven followed him upon white horses, clothed in fine linen, white and clean (Rev 19:11-14).

Compare the following description with the Man who wore a crown of thorns and bore His own cross under the whip to Calvary:

> And out of his mouth goeth a sharp sword, that with it he should smite the nations: and he shall rule them with a rod of iron: and he treadeth the winepress of the fierceness and wrath of the Almighty God (Rev 19:15).

There's no mistaking who it is at the head of that heavenly army: "And He hath on His vesture and on His thigh a name written, KING OF KINGS AND LORD OF LORDS" (19:16).

It's no contest. Revelation contains no scenes of lengthy battle. The Antichrist bit off more than he could chew.

We have seen the doom of the Antichrist and his assistant. "These both were cast alive into a lake of fire burning with brimstone," John reports (Rev 19:20).

And that's the end of the brief career of the man who declared himself God.

10

The End Times—A Timetable

DOES THIS CHAPTER title make you think of those cartoons of bearded men waving signs saying, "Repent, the end is near?"

Are we who search Scripture for knowledge of the future going to shout out that same hackneyed message?

We certainly are! We must!

Judging from certain Scriptures which give the characteristics of "the end times," the end is indeed near. Should you make your peace with God at this time? Yes. Today would be better than tomorrow. This afternoon would be better than this evening.

The Bible does not give a date for the end of this world for good reasons. If it did we would certainly tell it to you, and you would certainly do whatever you had to do to avoid the consequences. Then God would have collected a massive flock of sheep, blind sheep who followed out of plain fear.

Belief is the ticket out of all this. The Scriptures are designed to inspire faith.

First, in discussing what's to come, let us look at the timetable of events given in the Scriptures.

THE SCHEDULE OF EVENTS

First will come the rapture. This is the moment when

FUTURE TIMETABLE OF BIBLE PROPHECY

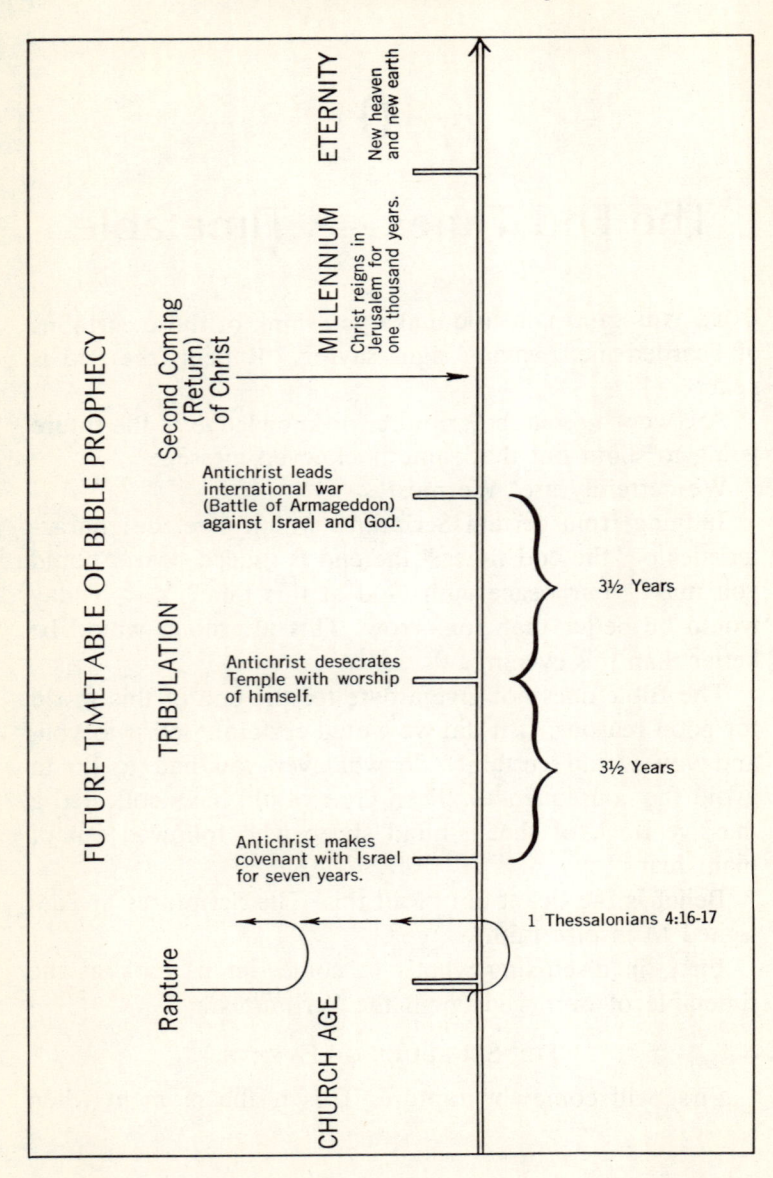

CHURCH AGE

Rapture — 1 Thessalonians 4:16-17

TRIBULATION

- Antichrist makes covenant with Israel for seven years.
- 3½ Years
- Antichrist desecrates Temple with worship of himself.
- 3½ Years
- Antichrist leads international war (Battle of Armageddon) against Israel and God.

Second Coming (Return) of Christ

MILLENNIUM — Christ reigns in Jerusalem for one thousand years.

ETERNITY — New heaven and new earth

The End Times—A Timetable

Christ will claim His sheep from the earth—the dead first (those who died believing) and then the living. Believers will go with Him and thus avoid the following events.

Next will come the tribulation.* This is the period of seven years prophesied by Daniel during which the Antichrist will occupy the Jerusalem Temple and proclaim himself to be God. The period will begin with his ingratiating peace proposal for Israel. The self-deification will be after three and one-half years. The Antichrist will reign for another three and one-half years, and then the great war will break out.

The battle of Armageddon, the next event, is the war to end all wars. This one is so terrible that the Lord observed that if He did not shorten those days there would not be a single survivor. This was beyond the imagination of those on the scene, but we of the megaton-bomb civilization do not have to stretch our minds to picture a war that would devastate the entire planet.

The fourth event is the triumphant return of Christ— this time as a lion instead of a lamb. He will establish His own Temple and proceed to reign over the earth's happiest thousand years.

After this millennial kingdom, Satan will have a last chance at corrupting the earth but will fail (Rev 20:7-8). Evil will be destroyed on the earth once and for all.

Then comes the period called eternity. Eternity will require a new earth, a new heaven, and a new Jerusalem. The changes are not within our powers of imagination, but apparently this refurbished model of creation is one that will endure in peace and triumph forever. It will be peopled by those who have the eternal life given by Jesus.

---

* The term *the tribulation* is commonly applied by prophetic students to the entire seven-year period of the Antichrist's covenant with Israel. The Bible uses the term prophetically only once—see Matthew 24:21, 29.

THE RAPTURE

The rapture is the moment the Lord will take His church—the Christians—off the earth to join Him in heaven (1 Th 4:16-17). The rapture is not some hopeful philosophy to help the Christians endure the trials of earthly life; it is a specific promise from Christ Himself.

The Lord told his nervous disciples at the Last Supper: "Let not your heart be troubled: ye believe in God, believe also in me. In my Father's house are many mansions. . . . I go to prepare a place for you. . . . I will come again, and receive you unto myself; that where I am, there ye may be also" (Jn 14:1-3).

From that moment on, Christians have awaited the Lord. The rapture is the gateway into eternal bliss, which Christ promised to all believers. It will spare the church—the body of believers—the cataclysmic events of the tribulation period and Armageddon. It is the great fulfillment of those who have followed Jesus Christ.

What about those Christians of ages gone by who faithfully awaited the Lord but died on earth?

> We which are alive and remain unto the coming of the Lord shall not prevent [go before] them which are asleep. For the Lord himself shall descend from heaven with a shout, with the voice of the archangel, and with the trump of God: and the dead in Christ shall rise first: then we which are alive and remain shall be caught up together with them in the clouds, to meet the Lord in the air: and so we shall ever be with the Lord (1 Th 4:15-17).

First Corinthians 15:51-55 reveals an interesting detail. There will be a metamorphosis—a mysterious change—in the bodies of the believers when they are raised. The Lord Himself underwent such a change for His own resurrection. The physical nature of the believers is to be outfitted for immortality:

> Behold, I show you a mystery; we shall not all sleep, but we shall all be changed, in a moment, in the twinkling of an eye, at the last trump: for the trumpet shall sound, and the dead shall be raised incorruptible, and we shall be changed. For this corruptible [flesh] must put on incorruption, and this mortal [body] must put on immortality. Then shall be brought to pass the saying that is written, Death is swallowed up in victory [Is 25:8]. O death, where is thy sting? O grave, where is thy victory?

Like the Lord Himself, the Christians will defeat death.

So, a trumpet will sound, the Lord will return, and the church will be saved from disaster.

Hal Lindsey refers to the rapture in *The Late, Great Planet Earth* as "the ultimate trip." It certainly is. It's the only way to go.

On the prophetic timetable, the rapture comes before the Antichrist's desecration of the Tribulation Temple. It must precede his proclaiming himself God.

The Tribulation Temple could be built before the rapture, of course. It could theoretically stand for centuries before the rapture and subsequent take-over by the Antichrist.

But if we may consider God's plan for a moment—it looks as if things are building up for Armageddon. Temple plans are being discussed; the heat is on in the Middle East like it never has been before; Russia is on the scene; and we can feel the worldwide tension. This would be a logical moment for the Antichrist to step in with his solution for the crisis in Israel.

Let's put it this way: if the rapture came right now—before you finished reading this sentence—and the Temple site were to be cleared and a new Temple put up in the next three years; and Armageddon (World War III) were to come about after seven years, it would not surprise Christians.

That would put the Messianic kingdom at ten years from today.

Ready?

THE TRIBULATION

This is the seven-year period marked by the entrance of the Antichrist into world affairs. He won't look like an Antichrist when he first appears, of course. In fact, his workable Middle East solution and his generally endearing personality will cause him to be regarded as a great statesman. And perhaps at the beginning he really will seem to be a warm and loving leader.

But it will not take long—three and one-half years in fact—for his powerful position to go to his head. He will enter the Temple and put a stop to the sacrifices and oblations, claiming that he should be the one to be worshiped. He will finish out the tribulation period—three and one-half more years—virtually ruling the earth.

But in the end he will not get the adulation he counted on. He will get Armageddon.

So, the tribulation runs from the first entrance of the Antichrist to the great war—a seven-year span.

Where does the third Temple stand in all this? Right on its famous site in Jerusalem. It must be standing there for the Antichrist to desecrate.

The End Times—A Timetable

The prophet Daniel regretfully foresaw all of this: "He shall confirm the covenant with many for one week [seven years]: and in the midst of the week he shall cause the sacrifice and the oblation to cease. . . even until the consummation [Armageddon]" (Dan. 9:27).

The Lord corroborated this, as we have seen, and added some good advice about those terrible times.

> When ye therefore shall see the abomination of desolation, spoken of by Daniel the prophet, stand in the holy place, (whoso readeth, let him understand:) then let them which be in Judea flee into the mountains: let him which is on the housetop not come down to take anything out of his house: neither let him which is in the field return to take his clothes. . . . For then shall be great tribulation, such as was not [seen] since the beginning of the world to this time, no, nor ever shall be (Mt 24:15-21).

ARMAGEDDON

No use going into a lot of detail about this event. In the old days, when people fought with the blade and the torch, commentators must have had a hard time getting them to realize the full horror of Armageddon. Scriptures about "fire down from heaven" were regarded as referring to devine retributions—not napalm bombs and nuclear fission. That the whole earth might be involved in a single war would have amazed even the generations who saw our previous world wars.

But in the holocaust that's coming, we are apparently going to use the sum total of man's vast, deadly war-making knowledge. Jesus Christ will finally hasten to the scene because, "except those days should be shortened, there should no flesh be saved" (Mt 24:22).

For our purposes in looking at the story of the Tribulation Temple, Armageddon marks its ending point. Jerusalem will be the scene of such mass killing and pillage that it would sicken Nebuchadnezzar. The Temple must fall. But its replacement will be the most important building ever to grace this planet. The Millennial Temple, the fourth and final Jerusalem Temple, will be the house of the Lord on earth, literally. Christ will reside in His Temple, built, of course, on that special mountain "which I will show to thee."

The prophet Zechariah places Armageddon in Israel, its focal point, with Jerusalem particularly involved. "I will gather all nations against Jerusalem to battle; and the city shall be taken, and the houses rifled, and the women ravished; and half the city shall go forth into captivity" (Zec 14:2).

Revelation gives Armageddon its name, from the site of the ultimate battle. "They are the spirits of devils . . . which go forth unto the kings of the earth and of the whole world, to gather them to the battle of that great day of God Almighty. And he gathered them together into a place called in the Hebrew tongue Armageddon" (Rev 16:14-16).

"Armageddon" refers to the Mount of Megiddo in Israel where countless bloody battles have been fought. A valley, called the Valley of Jehoshaphat by the prophet Joel, reaches from the mountain westward to the port of Haifa. It is a fine place for a first class war. Joel predicted it very clearly:

> Proclaim this among the nations; prepare war; stir up the mighty men; let all the men of war draw near, let them come up. . . . Haste ye, and come, all ye nations round about, gather yourselves together: thither cause thy mighty ones to come down, O Jehovah. Let the nations bestir themselves, and come up to the valley of Jehosha-

phat. . . . Multitudes, multitudes in the valley of decision! For the day of Jehovah is near in the valley of decision (Joel 3:9-14 ASV).

THE RETURN OF CHRIST

The day of the Lord will be near indeed as events progress in the valley of decision. Men will have the means to destroy their entire race at once, not slowly as at present, but the Lord will come and prevent this.

Past commentators had to use a lot of imagination in describing the Lord's actual reappearance since Revelation tells us: "Behold, he cometh with clouds; and every eye shall see him" (1:7).

How can every eye on earth see Him at once?

An intriguing possibility, hitched again to our modern times and our concept of things, is satellite television. The image of Christ would indeed be beamed on the clouds, and accessible to every eye at once.

If you thought His return (the second coming) was being televised live, would you turn on your set?

But the Lord will not be coming as a TV personality. Instead, His coming will have a grim purpose, as we have seen. Revelation describes Christ's dealing with the powers at the bloody work of Armageddon. John writes:

> And I saw heaven opened, and behold a white horse; and he that sat upon him was called Faithful and True, and in righteousness he doth judge and make war . . . and his name is called The Word of God [see Jn 1:1,14]. . . . And he hath on his vesture and on his thigh a name written, KING OF KINGS AND LORD OF LORDS (Rev 19:11-16).
>
> And I saw the beast [the Antichrist], and the kings of

the earth, and their armies, gathered together to make war against him that sat on the horse, and against his army (19:19).

The Lord and His heavenly troops ("Upon white horses, clothed in fine linen, white and clean" 19:14) dispose of the forces of the Antichrist. We owe the fire-and-brimstone religious terms to this accounting of the final moment of Armageddon: "And the beast was taken, and with him the false prophet.... These both were cast alive into a lake of fire burning with brimstone" (19:20).

Zechariah also wrote about this incident, supplying the fact that an earthquake will split the Mount of Olives:

> Then shall the LORD go forth, and fight against those nations.... And his feet shall stand in that day upon the mount of Olives, which is before Jerusalem on the east, and the mount of Olives will cleave in the midst thereof toward the east and toward the west (Zec 14:3-4).

That may be how the Tribulation Temple is destroyed. The Mount of Olives stands just east of the Temple site, actually overlooking it. It is likely that the Temple site would suffer great damage from an earthquake so close by.

THE MILLENNIAL KINGDOM

Then, and only then, comes peace on earth, good will toward men. The race of men have done their all to destroy themselves and their world. Christ has come and put a stop to it.

Zechariah goes on triumphantly:

> And the LORD shall be king over all the earth: in that day shall there be one LORD, and his name one.... And men shall dwell in it, and there shall be no more utter

The End Times—A Timetable

destruction; but Jerusalem shall be safely inhabited (14:9-11).

> And it shall come to pass, that everyone that is left of all the nations which came against Jerusalem shall even go up from year to year to worship the King, the LORD of hosts, and to keep the feast of tabernacles (14:16).

Even the normally foreboding Isaiah sees idyllic scenes of peace:

> The wolf also shall dwell with the lamb, and the leopard shall lie down with the kid; and the calf and the young lion and the fatling together; and a little child shall lead them. And the cow and the bear shall feed; their young ones shall lie down together; and the lion shall eat straw like the ox. And the suckling child shall play on the hole of the asp [snake den], and the weaned child shall put his hand on the cockatrice' den.
>
> They shall not hurt nor destroy in all my holy mountain: for the earth shall be full of the knowledge of the LORD, as the waters cover the sea (Is 11:6-9).

Isaiah corroborates Zechariah's picture of world worship in Jerusalem, and lasting peace:

> And it shall come to pass in the last days, that the mountain of the LORD's house shall be established in the top of the mountains ['Upon one of the mountains which I will tell thee of. . .'], and shall be exalted above the hills; and all nations shall flow unto it. And many people shall go and say, Come ye, and let us go up to the mountain of the LORD. . . . and they shall beat their swords into plowshares, and their spears into pruninghooks: nation shall not lift up sword against nation, neither shall they learn war any more (Is 2:2-4).

At this time Christ awards a place in the new kingdom to the believers who died during the tribulation: "I saw the souls of them that were beheaded for the witness of Jesus [executed for their belief in Jesus], and for the word of God, and which had not worshipped the beast . . . and they lived and reigned with Christ a thousand years" (Rev 20:4). Those who died in unbelief miss out on that splendid millennium: "But the rest of the dead lived not again until the thousand years were finished" (20:5).

Satan will be bound inactive during that thousand-year period, according to Scripture, but he will rise up again at the end of the millennium for one last try at spoiling the peace of the earth. But he, too, ends up in the lake of fire.

Then comes the famed judgment day (Rev 20:11-15) where all unbelievers will get their rewards according to their deeds. The book of life will be opened and everyone will be judged. Those not appearing in this *Who's Who of Salvation* will do no better than the devil and his handymen: "And whosoever was not found written in the book of life was cast into the lake of fire (20:15).

ETERNITY

And here is the last chapter in creation. Eternity will involve the metamorphosis of earth, heaven, and Jerusalem. For one thing there will be no more oceans:

> And I saw a new heaven and a new earth: for the first heaven and the first earth were passed away; and there was no more sea. And I John saw the holy city, [the] new Jerusalem, coming down from God out of heaven, prepared as a bride adorned for her husband (Rev 21:1-2).
> Of old hast thou laid the foundation of the earth: and the heavens are the work of thy hands. They shall perish, but thou shalt endure: yea, all of them shall wax old like a garment; as a vesture shalt thou change them, and they

The End Times—A Timetable

shall be changed: but thou art the same, and thy years shall have no end (Ps 102:25-27).

Those will be the days!

God shall wipe away all tears from their eyes; and there shall be no more death, neither sorrow, nor crying, neither shall there be any more pain: for the former things are passed away. And he that sat upon the throne said, Behold, I make all things new. And he said unto me, Write: for these words are true and faithful (Rev 21:4-5).

And what about the Temple site? Is there a new Temple? Is the concept of a special site and a special Temple to be forgotten now, after all of earth's history since Abraham, plus the millennial kingdom?

Not at all. The apostle John purposely considers it when he is shown the New Jerusalem, and he gives the final statement on this great theme of God's plan: "I saw no Temple therein [in Jerusalem]: for the Lord God Almighty and the Lamb are the temple of it" (Rev 21:22).

We might say that all along the Temples were symbolic of God and His Son, for they now personally replace them.

How to Use this Timetable

Your use of the timetable depends on your position with God. If you have received Christ, simply await the rapture and go to be with God. Pray with John, "Amen. Come Lord Jesus." (Bible: last page)

If you are not a believer, things are a bit more complicated. Step one is to watch for the construction of the Tribulation Temple. When that happens, the stage is set for earth's final act. The rapture may come before or after it. In any case, look for a mysterious disappearance of the Christians. They'll be here today and gone tomorrow.

When the Temple is up, watch for the Antichrist. We've described him earlier. His appearance will likely mark the beginning of your final seven years.

When you see him desecrate the Tribulation Temple, start your bomb shelter and cancel your insurance. Then Armageddon will be three and a half years off, and you might as well keep your head down.

You may survive the Armageddon. If so, watch for Christ to come; this will likely be a thrilling moment whatever your philosophy.

It's unclear what will happen to you next. But you do have one more appointment, whether you die a natural death or are one of the casualties of the Armageddon.

You'll get a subpoena; you'll have to appear before Christ on judgment day.

11

The Truth Will Set You Free

AT THE TRIAL OF JESUS CHRIST, Pontius Pilate asked a nagging question which has been on the minds of men from time immemorial.

Jesus had identified Himself for His earthly judge by testifying, "For this cause came I into the world, that I should bear witness unto the truth. Every one that is of the truth heareth my voice" (Jn 18:37).

Pilate, having difficulty seeing this mild-mannered young preacher as a danger to the state, asked the Lord "What is truth?"

We have an advantage over Pilate in our times. We have the Bible and many history books. We can compare prophecy with history and see plainly what is true. Our advantage comes in our having seen more prophecy fulfilled than Pilate could have. For example, we have seen the destruction of the second Temple, as prophesied, and the regathering of Israel, as prophesied.

But it wouldn't have been Pilate's style to look into Old Testament prophecy. A man who had advanced to an esteemed position in the complex Roman hierarchy would certainly have been more concerned with the things of the world than the things of heaven. The tendency is still very prevalent.

Today's educated unbeliever is Pilate's descendent in his unconcern for biblical truth. This world has grown ever more worldly since Pilate's occupational government. That expedient jurist would be really impressed to see our politics, our courts, our weapons, and our wars.

And, pathetically, we are still asking in so many ways, "What is truth?"

What is the truth about man's inhumanity to man? What is the truth about our ever-expanding wars? What is the truth about the end of the world?

Through this book, we have tried to illuminate the truth. We have quoted the Scriptures exactly. We have considered the accuracy of past prophecy and compared the observations of biblical personalities who lived many centuries apart. We have followed the extraordinary history of the Jerusalem Temple site from Genesis to Revelation. We have seen that God's Word has been utterly accurate to date.

We see no reason for that accuracy to stop now.

As of the recapture of the Temple site by the Jews in the 1967 war, the world divided into two camps—those with God and those without. There always have been these two camps, but never so unreasonably as now. Now the Tribulation Temple can be built. Now the Antichrist can come forward. Now the Armageddon can happen. Now Christ can return.

And now we can see God's plan unfolding.

It is unreasonable for the world still to be in two camps, because we can now see the truth.

We have the chance of Pilate; we can look truth in the face.

The Truth Will Set You Free

It won't happen, unfortunately, that all the world will turn to God now. Even as His last act progresses, many will watch the play in unbelief.

People will not believe when they see the foundation laid for the Tribulation Temple. They will not believe when the rapture occurs. It will be interesting to see the reasons formulated for the remarkable disappearance of the Christians.

They will not believe when the Antichrist comes forward, desecrates the Temple, and brings on the Armageddon.

And Jesus Christ will return to a world of unbelievers.

How sad. When the Lord, who suffered so for our redemption, comes back to the world, He will be surrounded by those who would not even pick up the receipt.

How disappointed the Lord was after He healed the ten lepers. When only one came back to thank Him, He said wistfully, "Were there not ten cleansed?"

The believers have a big job on their hands now. The world cannot be saved. As Jesus pointed out time and again, "It is written."

But *some* people can be saved. The divine attitude is clear: "The Lord is . . . not willing that any should perish, but that all should come to repentance" (2 Pe 3:9).

The believers must go forward now as never before and harvest the Lord's fields. The world has not gotten any easier to reach since the ministries of the apostles, but time is running out. Mass media, the churches, and every available device must be pressed into service to bring the truth to the unbelieving world.

And one-to-one witnessing, as utilized by Jesus Christ, must flourish in this degenerating world.

For the unbeliever the issue is clear. Go to God now. He

awaits you. He said, "I stand at the door, and knock" (Rev 3:20).

If the issues in this book bring up any kind of question in your mind, search it out. Check the prophets. Look up the Scriptures. Watch the newspapers for God's plan developing.

Don't make a hasty decision about this issue. Don't throw it out summarily. Remember Jeremiah's trial. They thought he was a crank.

Going to God is simple. It's natural—as natural as a thing can be—since it is the plan of the Maker of nature. Speak to God; He hears. Use your own words and your own thoughts; He knows them.

The truth will set you free.

Don't wait for the Temple site events to convince you. Remember that the rapture may come at any moment. Nothing has to precede the rapture of God's people. It would be a shame to miss the rapture and be here for the rest of the unhappy ending.

Don't wait to see if this book is accurate. If you wait to prove that we are telling the truth, you will find yourself in the unfortunate position of King Zedekiah, who ignored Jeremiah's warnings. He sat in a Babylonian jail while the Temple burned.

But the truth will set you free.

As soon as you are saved—as soon as you have turned to God—get on with the harvest! Help spare your friends and neighbors the agonies to come. Witness for our Lord. He will use you if you will be used. He said, "Go . . . and make disciples of all nations" (Mt 28:19, NASB).

And pray. Pray for this failing old world. Pray with us:

Dear God, merciful and just, it is not for us to know Your times and seasons. But You did give us Your Word, and

The Truth Will Set You Free

we have read it and put it away in our hearts. We can see Your new Temple of Jerusalem already in the minds of men. We know its significance in Your plan. We see the fulfillment of the words of Your prophets. We see the terrible Armageddon. We know You will fulfill Your plan as You always have.

Lord, You have provided cleansing for us all but so few have returned to acknowledge it. For those who went their own way and have disregarded the sacrifice of Jesus Christ, we pray. We will go and make disciples. We ask Your strength and mercy in this task.

And we ourselves, Lord, thank You a thousand times over. We await our Lord with confidence and joy. Amen. Come, Lord Jesus.

Notes

CHAPTER 2

1. "Eschatological Stirrings: Madman at the Mosque?" *Christianity Today,* February 27, 1970, p. 35.
2. Sinai Halberstam, "The Beth Hamikdosh," *The Jewish Press,* August 2, 1968, p. 19.
3. "Should the Temple Be Rebuilt?" *Time,* June 30, 1967, p. 56.
4. Ibid.
5. Ibid.
6. Victor Smadja, ed., *Yanetz Prayer Letter* 10 (July 1972): 1-2.
7. *New Scofield Reference Bible,* p. 918.
8. John F. Walvoord, *Israel in Prophecy* (Grand Rapids: Zondervan, 1962, p. 125; *New Scofield Reference Bible,* pp. 883, 888; Charles Lee Feinberg, *The Prophecy of Ezekiel* (Chicago: Moody, 1969), p. 237.
9. *The Jewish Encyclopedia,* s.v. "Cohen."

CHAPTER 3

1. *Jerusalem Post,* Feb. 10, 1976. Used by permission.
2. *Jerusalem Post,* Aug. 8, 1973. Used by permission.
3. *Jerusalem Post,* March 16, 1976. Used by permission.
4. *Jerusalem Post,* Feb. 17, 1976. Used by permission.
5. *Jerusalem Post,* March 21, 1976. Used by permission.
6. *Jerusalem Post,* March 9, 1976. Used by permission.
7. *Jerusalem Post,* March 23, 1976. Used by permission.
8. *Dallas Morning News,* March 22, 1976.
9. *Jerusalem Post,* April 6, 1976. Used by permission.

CHAPTER 4

1. George Cornell, "Second Coming Linked to New Jewish Temple." Used by permission of the Associated Press.
2. Ibid.
3. Committee for the Erection of the Jerusalem Great Synagogue, *The Jerusalem Great Synagogue.*
4. Ibid.
5. Ibid.

Chapter 5

1. Mordecai HaCohen, "The Rebuilding of the Temple—Jewish Views," *Christian News from Israel* n.s. 22, no. 1, pp. 10-11.
2. Ibid.
3. Harry J. Zuckerberg, *On the Study of the Bible Without the Book* (Flushing, N.Y.: Inst. of Bible Design, 1972), pp. 111, 113.
4. Ibid., pp. 117-18.

Chapter 6

1. John F. Walvoord, *Israel in Prophecy*, p. 97.
2. Sir Robert Anderson, *The Coming Prince* (Grand Rapids: Kregel, 1967), pp. 122-28.

Chapter 7

1. Josephus *Wars of the Jews* 5.9.4.563.
2. Ibid.
3. Ibid.

Chapter 8

1. Gabriella Rosenthal, *Jerusalem* (Garden City, N.Y.: Doubleday, 1968), p. 35.
2. Josephus *Wars of the Jews* 5.5.6.555.
3. Solomon H. Steckoll, *The Gates of Jerusalem* (New York: Praeger, 1968), p. 40.
4. Josephus 6.3.4.5.79.
5. Ibid., 5.1.4.548.